Coaching Presence

For Ash
And for all coaches who want to be a better
coach tomorrow than they are today.

Coaching Presence

Building consciousness and awareness in coaching interventions

Maria Iliffe-Wood

KoganPage

LONDON PHILADELPHIA NEW DELHI

First published in Great Britain and the United States in 2014 by Kogan Page Limited

2nd Floor, 45 Gee Street
London EC1V 3RS
United Kingdom

1518 Walnut Street, Suite 1100
Philadelphia PA 19102
USA

4737/23 Ansari Road
Daryaganj
New Delhi 110002
India

www.koganpage.com

ISBN   978 0 7494 7057 9
E-ISBN   978 0 7494 7058 6

British Library Cataloguing-in-Publication Data

A CIP record for this book is available from the British Library.

Library of Congress Cataloging-in-Publication Data

Iliffe-Wood, Maria.
   Coaching presence : building consciousness and awareness in coaching interventions / Maria Iliffe-Wood.
      pages cm
   ISBN 978-0-7494-7057-9 (pbk.) – ISBN 978-0-7494-7058-6 (ebk) 1. Personal coaching. 2. Counseling. I. Title.
   BF637.P36.I45 2014
   658.3'124–dc23

                                                      2013037264

Typeset by Amnet
Printed and bound in India by Replika Press Pvt Ltd

CONTENTS

ACKNOWLEDGEMENTS

I would like to thank a number of key people who have helped me with this book.

First of all thank you to Ashley Wood, without whom this book would not exist. Thank you so much for your love, your unwavering support and never ending patience. Thank you also to Rose Schofield, who has been with me since the beginning of the book. Thank you to both of you for being such great critical friends and for challenging me to stretch my thinking.

Thank you also for the feedback and lovely positive encouragement along the way from Mandy Hunt, Colin Wilson and Gilly Freedman.

Thank you to all my family and friends who have so patiently allowed me to be a recluse while writing this book.

Finally I have been lucky enough to have three key influencers in my coaching and supervision career. Thank you to all three of you: Rose Schofield, William Pennington and Nick Smith.

ABOUT THIS BOOK

From little acorns…

One day in 2012 I was driving along with the radio on. I don't remember much about the journey. I wasn't really paying attention to the radio but I heard the word 'invisible'. And I thought to myself, 'invisible coach?' In that moment the germ of an idea was born. This germ prompted me to undertake a process of critical evaluation of my own coaching practice and this book is the result.

I was in the habit of reflecting on my coaching work and I started to use the word 'invisible' as a foundation stone for my reflections. For each session I identified all the component parts of my coaching: preparation, structures, interventions, including my reasons for using interventions and anything else that was going on in my head at the time. It became apparent through this reflection and evaluation that being invisible was a good way to describe a significant element of my coaching – a thread that ran through the whole thing, but it was by no means the full story. I continued analysing my coaching and eventually I identified that I use four distinct modes. In each mode my approach with the client is very different and what determines each mode is my intention for the client's learning; it was all to do with clients accessing their own levels of awareness (discussed later). The germ became an acorn. I started sharing my thinking with other coaches and realized that these four distinct modes are related to this illusory and almost indefinable thing we call 'coaching presence'. I developed these four modes into a model and this forms the core of this book.

Why this book?

My hope in writing this book is that it will help you to develop your coaching presence at a faster pace than I did. That's not to say that I am a fully mature coach, or that I have all of the answers, far from it: I still consider myself a work in progress. What I do have is a level of experience and maturity that puts me in a position to help enough people to reach the stage that I have reached in my coaching.

I have put my own practice under the microscope so that I can write this for you. In doing so it has already helped me to develop my presence, my coaching relationships, my practice, my self-awareness and my maturity and I see greater transformation happening in my clients. This makes me really optimistic that this way of thinking about coaching presence can help you to move forward with yours while I continue on with my journey.

The context that I come from in writing this book is one-to-one coaching, primarily in a business setting, and one-to-one coach supervision. The principles transfer across to any kind of coaching including life, group or team coaching and consulting, mentoring or counselling and therapy. A counsellor/therapist friend of mine is already reflecting on her practice using principles from this book.

What this book offers

What this book offers is a way of thinking about your presence when coaching clients, which is paradoxical as the one thing we don't want to have to consciously think about is our presence. But as with all learning, first of all you need to know and understand the mechanics of it before it falls into unconscious behaviour, like learning to drive. And this book offers a way of thinking about the mechanics of coaching presence.

It will help you to think about how you are 'being' with your clients, to have the clients' best intentions at its heart and enable you to use all of your inner wisdom to be the very best coach that you can be. It's a way of being that enables you to create enough space in the coaching for you to draw on all of your learning, experience, knowledge, feelings, emotions, intuition and creativity (and anything else I've forgotten!) This in turn helps you to draw so much more from the client and results in a client who doesn't just grow but flourishes.

How the coaching relationship starts can make a significant difference to the success of the relationship. Chapter 1 is about laying the foundations for a successful coaching relationship, setting the scene for transformational learning to take place. How you contract with clients so that even before the coaching starts, they learn about how they are going to learn and how you are going to be with them. How you prepare yourself so that you can be fully present in the relationship and how you can help your clients to be fully present too. It also looks at ways in which you can use the environment to support this learning relationship.

In Chapter 2 I cover some of the personal factors that could be impacting, influencing or getting in the way of your coaching. This offers ways to explore and develop your own self-awareness. There is a lot of food for thought in this chapter, so be ready to spend some time reflecting on this. The chapter suggests a number of aspects for you to focus on so that you can work out how they might be impacting and what you might do about it.

The main body of this book – Chapters 3 to 6 – are structured in the same way. The model will help you build consciousness and awareness into your coaching interventions. It is a way of thinking in the moment about what you are trying to facilitate in the client, why you are doing so and how you are doing it. It offers you a structure to reflect on your coaching practice while you are coaching (Schön, 1991). At first it might sound like a lot to think about in the moment but the model can help to speed up decision making on interventions while taking into consideration what will facilitate the client's best learning in that moment. This model also provides a structure to enhance the learning that you might gain from your reflective practice.

Chapter 7 covers what I call 'channels of perception'. This relates to the myriad of ways in which you can help the client to surface new learning. It is as much to do with the methods of seeing new information as it is perspectives. In this chapter I encourage you to think about what channels of perception you are facilitating in the client with a view to expanding your range. The chapter offers very brief insights into a variety of interventions and might help you to identify some new learning avenues to bring into your coaching relationships.

The book finishes with how you might continue on your journey of self-discovery. It offers a structure to help you to achieve new learning from your reflective practice. It makes some suggestions about what you might do along this journey that will lead to great coaching presence, coach maturity and transformational coaching relationships.

How to use this book

Here's my recommendation for how to use this book so that it becomes a great learning experience for you:

1 Read one chapter at a time. Once you have read the chapter invest some reflective time in answering the questions at the end of the chapter.

2 Write in free flow about your thoughts and feelings about the answers to the questions. Draw some conclusions about how you might be different in your coaching relationships.

3 Identify one thing to change that you feel might make the most positive impact on your client's learning.

4 Find opportunities to practise this (see Chapter 8 for ideas about this).

5 Reflect on how it went and what the impact of this was on the client. Perhaps you can share with your client what you did differently and ask how it impacted on him or her.

6 Taking this into account, consider what you might do differently next time.

7 Consider what else you learnt in the chapter and how you might integrate this into your coaching practice. You can repeat 3–6 as often as you like.

8 Move on to reading the next chapter.

At the end of each chapter I will offer you some questions to use to reflect on the learning you might gain. In this learning experience I encourage you to be brave, take some risks, be interested and curious, take time to review and reflect and most of all enjoy the experience – all things I encourage in your coaching.

Professional coaching bodies

Much of the learning in this book will help you to develop the competencies that are recommended by the three main UK professional bodies. In the Appendix I detail how each chapter relates to these competencies.

Introduction

Coaching presence

To me the words 'coaching presence' suggest something of a higher quality and entirely different nature to just turning up and being there. It is a way of being. And this way of being will set the tone for the coaching. This way of being is significant to the degree of learning the client is able to achieve. Coaching presence is about creating an enabling space. Enabling for the client, enabling for the coach and enabling for the learning. What contributes to this way of being is a whole range of things.

First of all it is being 'in the moment' (Hall, 2013) with your client. You are not thinking about the past, nor worrying about the future: you are really interested and curious about what is happening right now. You are focusing all of your attention exclusively on this coaching relationship: that is all that is within, between and beyond the two of you in the wider system that encircles you and that relates to the client and his or her topic. You notice the nuances, and you wonder about what you notice.

You are both equal in the relationship and you value the diversity between you. You are respectful and trusting of the client and you make no judgements about him or her as a person. This valuing and respectfulness shine through in your being. You put aside your own needs for the duration of the coaching; they are not important. This includes setting aside your own personal factors (Chapter 2) as much as possible.

With compassion and empathy you hold a safe space for the client to express and deal with any difficult or uncomfortable issues. You are comfortable sitting with uncertainty and difficult emotions. You can help the client to sit with these and explore them without either of you getting drowned in the emotion. You are calm, fearless and mindful in helping your client to explore difficult issues.

You are fluid. You are flexible, adaptable and responsive to your client's needs. Your intuition and creativity comes to the fore to help the client. You flex and adapt any interventions that now form part of your unconscious competence (discussed in Whitmore, 2009). Things that you once had to concentrate on have now become second nature to you.

It is purposeful and deliberate. The purpose is the growth and actualization of the full potential of the client, and you both move towards this purpose by deliberateness in the coach, and deliberation by the client. Interventions are deliberately chosen by the coach, specifically for the purpose of the client's growth and learning, even when this deliberateness comes from unconscious competence. This is followed by deliberation by the client about the topic. In this presence you have time and space to reflect on your coaching practice; time to consider what you are doing, why you are doing it and your options while you are coaching (Schön, 1991).

Coach maturity

Coach maturity is intertwined with coaching presence: you are unlikely to develop one without the other. Coach maturity is not about age, or length of service; it is having a strong sense of 'who I am'; a strong sense of your own identity, particularly in the context of the coaching relationship. Mature coaches have a strong sense of purpose in the relationship and this is firmly embedded in the clients' learning. They work intuitively with their clients and they can draw on a wide diversity of interventions that come from a range of sources. They are self-aware, understanding what is impacting and influencing them and their interventions and how they are impacting on and influencing the client. They are aware of and bring into the coaching relationship the wider system and they create a dynamic energy in the room. Clutterbuck and Megginson (2010) describe this as the 'systemic-eclectic' coach.

Channels of perception

We are trying to help the client to access their inner wisdom and for me there are two key aspects. The first is to help clients 'to see what they cannot currently see' (Bachkirova, 2013). Most of what they cannot see is within their field of vision, but for whatever reason they just haven't noticed it yet. Our aim is to help them to notice these fields of vision by tuning into the myriad channels of perception that are always there, but which they have not yet explored.

The second aspect is the wider system of which they are just a small part. All parts of the system are interconnected and changes in one part will impact on other parts. Often solutions implemented either fail or cause other problems because clients have based their solution on a limited understanding of the whole system. Every time clients explore a new channel of perception they are likely to get a better understanding of another part of the system. It provides them with fresh insights. They access new, more or different information that will have a bearing on the topic they are exploring. As they look at it through a variety of channels they form a greater understanding of the whole system and this provides a more solid foundation for determining new ways of thinking and behaving. Any solutions have a greater chance of success when clients fully understand the topic. They have a greater understanding of the implications and consequences of any new action that they might be considering. The more channels of perception that are opened up for the client the greater the chance of him or her achieving transformational change.

So what are channels of perception? They are ways to view the topic and each one will raise new and different insights into the topic. I group these into two headings: people channels and interpretive channels, both of which I will explore in more detail in Chapter 7. Briefly, a people channel would be to look at the topic from one person's point of view, someone who is in the wider system. When you think about how many people this could be you can see that there are countless people channels that could be explored.

The interpretive channels are the various ways that people can make sense of their world. Using a metaphor is just one interpretive channel; another metaphor might open up another channel, so these too can be countless.

Levels of awareness

Before you choose which channel of perception you are going to invite the client to explore you need to know what it is you are trying to facilitate in the client. This is the 'level of awareness' you are hoping the client will access. This informs the mode of presence you will adopt. Once you know these then you choose the channel of perception.

The edges of these will be somewhat blurred but there are four possible levels of awareness (see Figure I.1):

1 What is obvious to the client – what's right in front of their eyes, so to speak.

2 What clients know at a deeper level and is harder for them to reach and recall, but is reasonably accessible.

3 What clients don't realize they know, have forgotten they know, or know but they are trying to avoid.

4 What clients don't know or they are unconsciously avoiding.

Each mode of presence will help you to access different level of awareness.

FIGURE I.1 The four levels of awareness

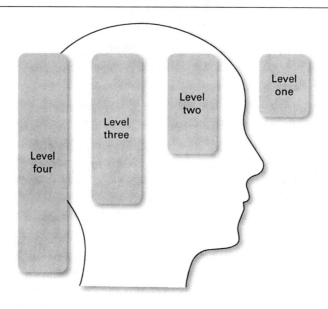

Guiding beliefs

Before I go on to explain the modes of presence I want to set out some guiding beliefs that underpin this framework (there are other beliefs specific to each mode and these will be mentioned in the relevant chapters). These guiding beliefs are broken down into three elements: what you believe about yourself, what you believe about the client, and what you believe about the coaching relationship. However, there is one belief that I believe supersedes all the others – the principal belief.

Principal belief

People can usually identify at least one person who was a key influence in their life. They might say that this person helped to shape them into the person they are today. With the help, guidance, support and encouragement of this person they were able to flourish. There are lots of other people we have met along the way who could have influenced us, but these particular people made a profound difference in our lives: there is something that marks them out from all the others.

When I think about what it was that marks out my key influencers it is just one thing: they believed in me. They had faith that I could achieve whatever it was I was working on and they trusted me to do it. They believed that I was capable of working things out for myself. I now carry this belief and because of this I have been privileged to see so many people realizing their potential.

So for me the principal belief above all the others is this:

Every person that I meet has a deep well of inner wisdom that they can tap into. I have faith that they can achieve whatever it is they are aiming for. I trust that they are genuinely striving to achieve it and that they can do it no matter how high the aspiration.

I know that at least some of you will be indignant about this statement. 'What if they are trying to achieve the impossible?' I've heard this many times when I talk about my principal belief. My answer is this: it's not up to me to decide that they can't do it! Someone once said to me, 'Well what if they say that they want to walk on water?' My response: 'How do I know that they are not going to be able to come up with a way of doing that?'

Think about this. It's 1896. Orville Wright has this idea about powered flight. It's never been done before but he wants to do it. In fact the whole world (apart from his brother and a smattering of others) believes it's impossible. He wants someone to help him work out how to achieve it. He's heard about coaching and has decided that's just what he needs, so he finds himself a coach. What would have happened if the coach, knowing that it is impossible to fly, coached him into finding something that was more realistic and achievable?

This may be surprising to you, but I have heard many coaches talking about their client's aspirations being too high or unrealistic or unachievable. The job of the coach is not to decide whether the client's aim is achievable or not. The job is to help the client to be sure and clear about what it is they want to achieve and then help them to work out what it will take to achieve it.

Guiding beliefs

So that's the principal belief but there are a few more that I think contribute to a great coaching relationship. These are grouped into beliefs about yourself, your client and the coaching relationship.

I am currently working with a client in her early 20s. She came to me with an idea about setting up a charity. We spent the first session exploring her goal. As I do with many of my clients, I helped her to visualize the end point. She worked out what this charity would be like when it was up and running how she intended it to be. What she came up with was a highly ambitious vision. We discussed a time frame and she realized that it is a long-term plan, perhaps 20 years or more. Both of us are excited about the prospect. I then helped her to work out what she needs to do now that will help her to achieve her ultimate goal. This includes doing small-scale charitable acts, developing her skills and building a network of contacts.

She is an inspiration to work with. I was telling a friend of mine about my client's vision (my client needs people to be aware of it). She remarked that this girl was lucky to have found me as a coach. It hadn't occurred to me before, but she's right. Another coach might have encouraged her to find something more 'realistic and achievable' to aspire to. Even if my client only achieves half of what she is aiming for, she will have created something very special. I am looking forward to being around to see it.

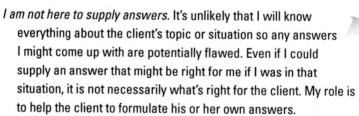

About yourself

Here's what I believe about myself:

I am not here to supply answers. It's unlikely that I will know everything about the client's topic or situation so any answers I might come up with are potentially flawed. Even if I could supply an answer that might be right for me if I was in that situation, it is not necessarily what's right for the client. My role is to help the client to formulate his or her own answers.

It's ok for me to not know. I don't need to know the whole story, or what the jargon means or the significance of what they are saying, or even really understand what they are talking about – as long as the client understands. If the client is continuing to explore then this is enough. When I choose interventions I do so with the intention of helping to expand the client's awareness, but I may not know *how* it will help or what the outcome will be.

I can put aside my own mental clutter (Whitworth *et al,* 2009). Whenever it presents itself I can choose to let go of it immediately. I am capable of recognizing when my personal factors are influencing my coaching and I can choose to be different.

I have faith in my intuition. I have used my intuition in the past and have often been proved right. Even when it has been slightly off it has usually been helpful in some way. I trust that I can use my intuition to help the client to find new channels of perception.

I have courage in my coaching. I am prepared to challenge my client's thinking in the interests of his or her learning. I can handle any emotional responses that this might stir up in the client.

I am the coaching expert. I am the person in the relationship who knows and understands how coaching works, and how it can help the client to learn and grow.

About the client

Here's what I believe about my clients:

Clients are whole persons. They are not broken and therefore they do not need fixing. They are fully functioning regardless of any physical limitations they may have. (Refer to Buckley and Buckley's 2006 guide when this proves not to be the case.) They are already highly capable and the aim is to build on this capability so that they can actualize their potential.

Clients learn best when they have worked things out for themselves. To learn and grow clients need to make their own connections (Schofield, 2009). Clients have the ability to think things through and work things out for themselves; their confidence will grow through using this ability and drawing their own conclusions. When I behave as if they can think for themselves they invariably do so.

Clients know much more than they think they know. It's amazing just how much information they have stored away that they don't even realize is there and how much wisdom they have inside themselves already if only they look for it and trust it. All it takes is some time and space for them to be able to access this.

I respect and value the client as a person. No matter what I think or feel about the client's behaviour I will always respect and value him or her as a person. Whatever the clients' point of view, it is valid for them, regardless of what I might think about it.

Clients are the expert on themselves and their system. Clients know the situation, the organization, the people involved much better than I do and therefore they are in a better place than me to draw conclusions, make judgements and work out any solutions. Clients are also the experts on themselves and they know best what the right decision is for them.

About the coaching relationship

Finally here's what I believe about the coaching relationship:

It is a collaborative experience. Both of us are equal in the relationship. Both parties bring different skills and knowledge to the relationship and have different responsibilities within it. The coach is responsible for facilitating the learning, the clients are responsible for their own learning. Both of us can learn and grow in the relationship.

There is a higher purpose for the relationship. The purpose of the coaching relationship is more than the stated aims of the coaching. It is more than finding solutions or helping the client to meet certain development needs. The higher purpose is the full actualization of the client's potential (Maslow, 1943). It's the difference between clients learning a new technique to manage a situation, and transforming something fundamental in their values and belief system so that they never have to use the technique again.

How we work together is as important as what we do. Clients will learn as much from how they learn in the coaching relationship as they do from the coaching itself. They learn about the skills that you use with them; skills that they can take away and use outside of the coaching relationship. They can use the interventions that you have used to help themselves or others to find new learning independently of you.

This relationship is highly important. The work that we do touches and impacts many lives, not just the lives of our clients. What they learn will make a difference to both their work and personal relationships. Changes in the client will facilitate changes in other people they deal with. They will be different with others, which will influence others to be different in some way. It means that this relationship has the power to positively impact on many lives, not just one.

Four modes of presence

What follows is explained in more detail in Chapters 3–6; here is a brief summary of the four modes of presence, shown in Figure I.2, which are:

1 Invisible Coach mode.

2 Emergent Coach mode.

3 Evident Coach mode.

4 Visible Coach mode.

Each mode of presence relates to how much of *you* is in the approach or intervention: how much you allow your thoughts, beliefs, opinions, judgements, feelings, etc to influence your work with the client. All of the modes of presence are designed to help clients access their own inner wisdom. You are helping clients to move deeper into their levels of awareness. Broadly the four modes translate across to the four levels:

- Invisible Coach mode – level one awareness.
- Emergent Coach Mode – level two awareness.
- Evident Coach Mode – level three awareness.
- Visible Coach Mode – level four awareness.

The modes of presence can be seen as a progression, but it is not a defined process. You are likely to move in and out of the modes, mixing them up and moving them around with Invisible Coach mode acting as a thread between all of them.

The model is built on the premise that you make a conscious and deliberate choice for every approach or intervention that you use with your client; eventually this becomes an unconsciously deliberate choice. You are mindful of what you notice in the client, how it lands with you and what's going to help the client in that moment. This model builds on and draws from

FIGURE I.2 The four modes of presence

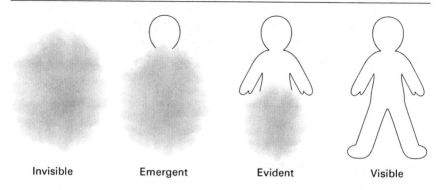

Invisible   Emergent   Evident   Visible

everything that you have learnt so far. What you do is representative of yourself, your awareness and your learning, that is your coach maturity.

Finally, each mode of presence comprises observably different behaviours. An observer of the relationship would be able to notice and distinguish which mode of presence you are using based on the different ways he or she sees you working with your client.

Here is a metaphor for the four modes of presence that I will come back to periodically. You (the coach) are the passenger in a car. The client is the driver. You both know the destination, or at least the approximate destination that you want to end up in:

- *Invisible Coach mode:* You trust the driver and enjoy the ride. You don't mind how you get to the destination. It's entirely up to the driver. But you are really interested in what's going on around you and most interested in what the driver is doing, which way he or she is going, how he or she is deciding which way to go.

- *Emergent Coach mode:* Now you offer the client a new map. Perhaps his or her existing map is an A–Z of the local area and the new one is an ordnance survey map of a bigger region. There is more information on the new map that can help the client determine which way he or she wants to travel.

- *Evident Coach mode:* Now you are taking a more active role in helping the client to choose how to get to the destination. You are highlighting different routes on the map, pointing out places of interest, and talking about what you experienced when you visited similar places. The driver still decides where he or she wants to go, and which route to take, but he or she is a bit more knowledgeable now and can make more informed choices.

- *Visible Coach mode:* You are now reading the map and giving the driver directions. You are quite insistent that the driver follows the route that you are suggesting; however the driver has control of the car and ultimately he or she decides which way to take it.

Invisible Coach mode

The key words for Invisible Coach mode are silence, listen, trust, patience, brevity, simplicity.

This is the mode where you are encouraging the client's own invisible coach to come to the fore. You are encouraging and waiting for the client to access their own inner wisdom and come up with their own learning.

You can also think of Invisible Coach mode as you being almost invisible to the client. Completely invisible does not help the client; completely invisible is absent. You have to be there to make a difference to the client's exploration (Kline, 1999; 2009). In this mode there is minimum coach input and maximum client input. You are offering the lightest of touches to the coaching.

You make a conscious decision to listen and pay attention to the client. To a degree you are letting go of the process and just seeing what happens. The client does the vast majority of the talking and you listen with interest and curiosity. The client takes the exploration wherever he or she wants to take it. During this time you notice things, but park (see the glossary in the Appendix) most of what you notice to draw on later.

Interventions will be very short and intermittent. They are simply an encouragement to the client to continue with his or her thinking. They follow the client's existing train of thought; you don't encourage the client to move into new directions. When you offer an intervention you are a mirror: the client only sees his or her own reflection. The interventions used will mostly involve replaying something back to the client.

The coach is not paying attention to any aspect of him or herself to inform the coaching. He or she is not trying to interpret or make meaning of anything the client is talking about, and is not reacting to anything the client says. The client is accessing his or her level one awareness, the uppermost layer of inner wisdom. You enjoy the client's resourcefulness.

On the face of it, Invisible Coach mode may seem to be the simplest of the four modes, but this doesn't mean it is the easiest. People often feel the need to fill the silence and some coaches will want to jump in quickly with interventions to move the coaching on. Waiting patiently and trusting the client to find his or her own way can be quite challenging, and you may feel like it goes against the grain of what you have learnt so far in your coach development. It might take practice before this mode feels as simple as it sounds.

Emergent Coach mode

The key words for Emergent Coach mode are stimulate, elevate, expand, magnify, detachment, creativity and perseverance.

When you are in Emergent Coach mode you are starting to take a slightly bigger role in the coaching. You are no longer just following the client's lead or acting as a mirror. You are stimulating some new thinking by providing the means for clients to look deeper within themselves. You are helping them to access their level two awareness.

Your level of input has gone up a notch. You are providing clients with new ways to notice and explore new channels of perception for themselves: channels that stretch their view, magnify the detail or elevate their perspective. They deepen the awareness from the client's own perspective, identify other people or interpretive channels and consider the topic through these channels. In doing so you are helping clients to reduce their bias in the exploration.

In Emergent Coach mode you might encourage the client to view the topic from a more detached or objective view. You might offer interventions that metaphorically or physically place the topic in the space between the two of you rather than inside the client's head. The topic becomes something tangible in the room and attention is focused on that, rather than focused inwards or on the coach. Your interventions are based on curiosity and interest about this 'entity' that is now in the space between you.

As with Invisible Coach mode you are not interpreting or making meaning of the client's exploration. The client is still choosing the direction of travel. What you are doing is providing him or her with a means of seeing the terrain differently. You are encouraging the client to use this new map as a way of enhancing his or her exploration. Emergent Coach mode is where you can be at your most creative in your interventions to expand the client's exploration.

Evident Coach mode

The key words for Evident Coach mode are share, inform, prompt, highlight and intuition.

In Evident Coach mode you are adding something of yourself to the coaching. You are using something of yourself to aid the client's exploration, not just providing a means to explore. You are showing or sharing aspects of yourself to the client. You will be clear that this is what you are doing. The client has the choice of whether to accept or reject this new data, which is very specific in nature. It does not include your opinions or suggestions. You are sharing aspects like feelings, emotions, images, words or phrases that are yours rather than the client's. You might share knowledge, or something from your experience.

Any data that you offer to the client is based on information that you are receiving from the client. Something about what the client is saying or doing tells you that it might be important or useful to share this information. This could be your intuition or can be more tangible aspects of the client's language.

The reason you share aspects of yourself is for the sole purpose of adding a new dimension to the client's exploration. It is likely to open up new channels of perception which help the client to access his or her level three awareness.

It is in Evident Coach mode where you are most likely to use and share your intuition. You might have a feeling and you don't know where it comes from or whether it's right or wrong but your 'gut' tells you that it is important.

Visible Coach mode

The key words for Visible Coach mode are steer, incite, probe, challenge, provoke and courage.

It is very clear when you are in Visible Coach mode: you are making your presence felt. In Visible Coach mode you are pushing the client, stirring things up. In the previous modes you calmly accepted it when the client rejected any of your interventions or information. In Visible Coach mode you don't make it so easy for him or her to reject these. The highest degree of coach input happens in Visible Coach mode.

In Visible Coach mode you are pressing clients to explore particular channels of perception. You are challenging them to extend the breadth and depth of their exploration. You have noticed what they have missed or avoided and you encourage them to explore these channels. It is always done with the best interests of the clients' learning in mind: you are helping them to access their level four awareness.

In Visible Coach mode you are likely to be taking clients out of their comfort zone into more difficult or emotional territory. You may be challenging them emotionally, ethically or legally. It takes courage, strength and determination, together with calmness and a surety that you are doing this in the clients' best interests.

In Visible Coach mode you are using more of your own views to inform the interventions. Your view is that there is potentially something important to learn from this channel or that the clients' thinking needs to change. There is the rare possibility that this will extend beyond the coaching as you may have to decide to involve relevant third parties as a result.

Some coaches may feel like Visible Coach mode is the one that comes most naturally although I venture that this is due to using this mode inadvertently and without full consideration. Using Visible Coach mode consciously with a clear intention of helping clients draw their own conclusions and to tap into their own inner wisdom is arguably the most difficult to master.

Hypothetical example

To try to demonstrate the difference between the modes here's an example of a situation that could arise in your coaching. I include four scenarios as options.

A client has said that she wants to explore a topic that (she says) is quite a challenge for her. She knows that it is likely to be difficult and it's not something she particularly wants to face but she knows that she needs to. The exploration has started and shortly into this she starts talking about something different that appears to be unrelated to the original topic. Here are the scenarios:

Invisible Coach mode: I notice the change in direction. I don't know how this is relevant to the topic that we are focusing on. I'm not sure if she is trying to dodge the difficult topic, but I trust that this is relevant and useful for her. I let her continue with the exploration.

Emergent Coach mode: I notice the change in direction. What she is talking about seems to be something different to the original topic but the same customers are involved. I invite her to consider the topic as a system, using objects to depict the various players in the system, bringing in both the original and new topic.

Evident Coach mode: I notice the change in direction. I also notice a change in myself. When she was talking about the difficult topic I felt quite tense, but now I feel quite relaxed. I share this change of feeling that I have just noticed in myself.

Visible Coach mode: My instincts tell me that she is trying to avoid the challenging topic. I have worked with her for a while and know her quite well. I trust my instincts. I interrupt this new exploration and ask how this is relevant to the topic that she said she wanted to work on today.

I'm sure you can think of other options but I keep it to four to demonstrate the difference between the four modes of presence.

Things to remember

Before you start coaching, make a conscious decision to remain present throughout the whole of the coaching session. You know that being absent for only a few seconds can mean missing something important the client is saying, missing an element of a pattern or a connection that might be important. Preparing yourself in the way that is discussed in Chapter 1 will give you the best chance of remaining present throughout.

The choice of mode of presence requires a deliberate decision. Each time you leave a mode you make another deliberate choice. Throughout the coaching regularly ask yourself two questions: 'Which level of awareness am I trying to facilitate in the client?' and, 'Which mode will help the client most in this moment?' Be definite about your choice. Once you have chosen the mode of presence, this will inform your interventions. It will immediately narrow or expand the options available to you or inform how you continue with an existing intervention.

The modes of presence can be used as a process but it is more likely that you will flow in and out of the modes, potentially using all of them frequently throughout the coaching session. You might come from multiple modes of presence for every intervention, or progress through the modes in one session or every variation in between. Each mode of presence enables the client to build on the learning gained through the previous mode. They can be used at any time and in any order. Invisible Coach mode acts as a thread that goes through the whole of the coaching. Regardless of your starting mode you fall back into Invisible Coach mode while clients follow the new train of thought and tap into their own inner wisdom.

There is always going to be some blurring around the edges. We are trying to define something that almost defies definition. The edges of the modes are like the brackish water where seawater meets fresh water. Seawater and fresh water exist in their own rights but in brackish water there can be any combination of both types. It is neither one nor the other.

You may find that you have a preference and a good level of skill in one or more of the modes, and feel uncomfortable with one or two of the others. To be the best coach that you can be you need to be competent in all four modes. While you could coach almost exclusively from each mode, in practice this would not be healthy for the client. Every mode has its advantages and disadvantages. However, to develop your competence in each of the modes you can practise (on a willing client) each mode separately.

There will be times when you use all of the modes inadvertently. This is when a particular mode is being used but you don't realize you are doing it. This doesn't make it wrong, although it might not be the most appropriate mode in the moment. Reflecting on these moments of inadvertent use of modes can provide valuable learning opportunities for you. Each chapter gives some suggestions about the ways in which the modes may be used inadvertently.

This framework should complement your learning so far. It is a way of thinking about how you apply the myriad of tools and techniques that you have in your repertoire and assimilating those that you have yet to learn into how you work with your clients.

Enjoy this learning experience.

Reflective questions

- Reading through the guiding beliefs, which of these most resonate with you? How does this currently impact on your coaching practice?

- Are there any guiding beliefs that you disagree with? How might this impact on your coaching practice? What would be an alternative belief that you could subscribe to? How might this impact on your coaching practice?

- Which of the four modes of presence do you feel most drawn to? Which do you feel instinctively comes more naturally to you?

- Which of the modes of presence do you feel most resistant to? What might this tell you about yourself?

Laying the foundations

01

In this chapter I highlight factors for you to consider that have the potential to enhance the learning experience and set the scene for a great coaching relationship. Paying attention to the topics discussed here will give your coaching relationship a head start.

I'll start with contracting. Often difficulties that arise in the coaching relationship later could have been prevented if they had been discussed in the initial contracting stage. This is relevant to many working relationships, not just coaching. I talk about how you can use the four modes of presence as a guide for your contracting process.

Next I talk about choosing a venue and then your location within the venue. These can have an impact, positive or negative, on the coaching relationship. Often we don't notice the impact a venue has on us when we walk into it, but it is there nonetheless. Understanding and taking account of this can make your job as a coach a bit easier.

I then offer you a process for preparing yourself for coaching sessions and a way to facilitate your client's presence in the relationship.

Contracting

Contracting is a broad subject so I am only talking about it in the context of the four modes of presence. I am not setting out everything to do with contracting; some of the books in the References and further reading chapter cover the contracting process (see Flaherty, 2005; Hawkins and Smith, 2006).

Using the modes of presence you will be working in four distinct ways with your clients. You contract with them in a way that helps them to appreciate and understand this so that there are no process surprises (hopefully there will be lots of learning surprises). Contracting in this way will help to ensure that if you need to have 'difficult' conversations with your client you have a foundation on which to base these discussions. For example, the client may ask for advice at a point in the coaching when you feel it is not appropriate to start sharing your experiences. You can refer back to your contracting discussion and then both decide how to proceed. That's a pretty straightforward example, but what if the client presents something in the coaching that presents you with an ethical dilemma? There's no easy answer to this dilemma, and there are a variety of options open to you. Some may be more difficult for you to introduce if you did not contract for these eventualities. (Handling ethics in coaching is covered in much more detail by Carroll and Shaw, 2013.)

Once you have an understanding of the four modes of presence you can use them to structure your contracting discussion, whether you are contracting with the client, the sponsor or the line manager. At the end of the contracting everyone should have a clear appreciation of the coaching relationship: they understand the roles and responsibilities and what they can expect. The client becomes aware of the possibilities for working and thinking differently in the sessions. It might give some people time to reflect on these and be more open to the idea when the time arises. The aim is that the contracting will clear a path for you to use all four modes of presence in your coaching relationship.

Start by discussing some of your guiding beliefs, what you believe about the client, your role and the coaching relationship. Once you have done that, here are some suggestions for what you might discuss under the heading of each mode.

Consider the following scenario.

You are being paid by an organization to coach a manager. You've coached him a few times and he is getting used to the idea of coaching. Next time you meet the manager checks with you that everything he discusses is confidential. He then announces that he wants you to coach him to leave the company. He plans to take some of his best clients with him and he's going to start a new company in competition with the organization. What do you do?

Invisible Coach mode

Talk about how much time they will spend talking while you listen and about how they will often determine their own line of thinking. Mention the fact that people you work with are often surprised that they have a much deeper knowledge of the subjects discussed than they realize. They will draw their own conclusions and formulate their own solutions and you are unlikely to provide them with suggestions. Clarify that it is your responsibility to draw out the answers that you know they already have within them, and it's their job to decide what they will then do with that information.

Emergent Coach mode

Talk about helping them to look at the topic from a wide range of perspectives, pointing out that doing this will help them shed new light on the subject and open up new solutions. Let them know about some of the wide variety of perspectives this might include (see Chapter 7). Also let them know that you might use some tools and techniques that they might perceive to be odd or unusual, but that these are designed to help them to think differently about the subject.

Evident Coach mode

Talk about when and how you might share aspects of yourself, what sorts of things you might share, and what you think might happen when you do this. Let them know how you might handle any requests for advice in the coaching relationship. Make it clear that when you share you do so with the intention of providing new information for them to explore and that they can choose whether to accept or disregard the information.

Visible Coach mode

Talk about how clients can expect to be taken out of their comfort zone, that you will encourage them to look at blind spots or aspects that they might be avoiding. Explain that you may challenge them to think about some things that might be difficult for them, including unsettling emotions. Explain that often when emotions become involved there is profound learning to be experienced and that where appropriate you will help them to work through these emotions with a view to achieving the learning.

When talking about what might happen, mention that ethical or legal considerations may arise and discuss with the client how you might handle these if it happens. This includes how you might handle situations where it becomes apparent that there might be an ethical or mental health issue. The hope is that you will never have to worry about these issues arising, but you can never say never. Discuss how you might proceed in these instances, which might include your seeking advice on the matter.

When you are contracting you are using Visible Coach mode. You are the expert on the subject of how you coach. Even where clients have had coaching before, they have not had coaching from you. Your style of coaching may be very different to others. You use your expertise to set the scene for clients. You help to prepare them for your style of coaching.

Choosing the environment

Where do you meet for the coaching sessions? The environment you work in can have an impact on the coaching. Often there is not a lot of choice in the matter but even when the choice is restricted, paying attention to environmental factors can have a positive impact on the coaching compared to not paying any attention at all. (If you use technology such as Skype or phone to coach, it is still worth paying this some attention.)

Encourage clients to make the decision about the venue. If you do this you are setting the precedent that they are the decision maker in this relationship. The clients get the message very early that you are not here to make decisions for them.

Why is it important?

Often attention is only paid to the environment when it gets in the way of what we are doing. For example, you might only notice how noisy a place is when you are trying to concentrate on something. It is best if the venue is not the cause of distractions. Having said that, I have coached in plenty of places where there have been lots of potential distractions and it has not got in the way. Things that often do get in the way are to do with comfort. A room that I have worked in occasionally has no natural light and the heating system is unreliable. People can work in it for only so long and then the room gets in the way: they get too hot or too cold and feel closed in. Throughout the session their attention moves away from the topic and towards their need for fresh air, or a change of temperature.

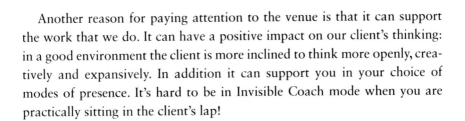

Walt Disney recognized how the environment helps to facilitate different thinking. He used separate rooms to work on different aspects of the development of his products (Dilts, 1994). All the rooms were different sizes and decorated and fitted out according to the activity that took place in that room – one room for creativity and idea generation, another for reality checking and another for critiquing and perfecting the product. Teams worked in the different rooms at the various stages, moving between the rooms several times before arriving at the final product. So take a leaf out of Walt's book and pay attention to the environment you are working in with your clients.

Another reason for paying attention to the venue is that it can support the work that we do. It can have a positive impact on our client's thinking: in a good environment the client is more inclined to think more openly, creatively and expansively. In addition it can support you in your choice of modes of presence. It's hard to be in Invisible Coach mode when you are practically sitting in the client's lap!

Facilitate the clients' choice of venue

There will be times when you have to make the decision about the venue, but make this the exception rather than the norm: encourage the client to make the decision. I say this with a caveat: use Visible Coach mode. As I mentioned in contracting, you are the expert on the coaching process. You are the one who knows what makes a good venue for coaching, so let them know what to look for. Provide some guidelines based on your expertise. Ask them to choose a venue taking these guidelines into consideration. Once they have made their choice, trust that it is the right choice for them. You're setting a precedent if you suggest a different venue after they have made their choice!

Sometimes there is only a very limited choice or no choice at all. There are times when other factors take precedence over choosing the ideal location, such as geography, travel restrictions, time, finances, topic sensitivity or access to data. If you are using a less than ideal location, two things spring to mind. First, give consideration to the environment in your preparation (discussed later in this chapter). Consider how the environment might impact on the coaching and therefore what steps can be taken to minimize the impact (eg extra breaks). Secondly, pay closer attention to choosing your position in relation to the client (also discussed later).

Environment factors

These are the factors that should be attended to when choosing a coaching environment. After listing them I will explain what I mean by them, not because it's complicated but because everyone makes their own meaning of statements.

The location should tick as many as the following items as possible:

- a place that is away from the distractions of the workplace;
- some distance between the workplace and the coaching venue;
- light and airy;
- spacious with a view, ideally a natural panorama;
- somewhere with a variety of seating options;
- room to move about;
- privacy and confidentiality.

Away from the distractions of the workplace

Ideally you need to work in a place where the coaching will not be interrupted by normal day-to-day activity. Obvious distractions such as people knocking on the door, the phone ringing, e-mails 'pinging' on the computer, paperwork, all demand attention. If you are in a venue away from these then you don't need to worry about the physical intrusion, although some clients bring potential distractions with them such as mobile phones and laptops.

It also needs to be away from the sights and sounds of the workplace. Often clients book a meeting room but you can still see and hear phones or people working, talking or walking by. Elements from outside the room attract attention that can prove difficult to ignore. What if the client is expecting a call from an important customer and the phone rings outside? You can see how easy it would be for him or her to be distracted. Also it needs to be a place where others who might be part of the topic cannot overhear.

Distance between the workplace and the coaching venue

A short physical journey from the workplace to the coaching venue gives the client time to make the mental journey from normal day-to-day work mode into coaching mode. The act of walking away from the work environment

Before I started paying attention to the venue I worked with a client in a meeting room adjacent to the area where her team was working. She took time to think about everything she said before she said it. It was the first session so it took a while for it to come to light that this was not her normal behaviour. Eventually she told me that she was worried that someone outside might overhear what she was saying. The room was not soundproof. We resolved to change venue for future sessions.

can provide some mental distance. Clients are no longer in the thick of it so they can see it more objectively.

The short journey back also provides some space for clients to reflect on the session and gives the learning time to settle in their mind before they have to focus all of their attention back on the day-to-day activity. Putting some distance between the work environment and the coaching venue addresses the issue of work distractions, it can help to move the client into a coaching way of thinking, and it can provide time for the client to embed the learning.

Light and airy

A place that has plenty of natural light and fresh air can be really helpful for a productive coaching session. Walk into a room with air conditioning and artificial lighting and almost immediately we can feel closed in and constricted. Walk into a room with fresh air and natural light and it feels open and more welcoming, and this impacts on our minds and how we think. The natural light and fresh air seem to help to lift the spirits, relax and open our minds and as a result it feels easier to think clearly and be creative.

Spacious with a view

Have you noticed how when people are talking they look everywhere except at the person they are talking to? And where they look appears to make a difference to what they are thinking (or is it that they look in a different place when their thinking changes)?

(Note: It is not something that I have studied, but I am aware of the fact that in neuro linguistic programming they talk about eye-accessing cues which might relate to what I am talking about here; see Knight, 2009 or O'Connor and Lages, 2004.)

I noticed this when I was in a session with my supervisor. We were in a public meeting area and I noticed a correlation between my thinking and where my eyes rested in and around the room. I would look up to the far corners of the room, or out of the windows when I was looking for inspiration. I looked towards different things in the room at different times in my exploration. There wasn't a view of nature from this place but it was a beautiful and interesting building. There was lots of artwork around, and sculptures and designs built into the walls. The beauty and interesting artefacts coupled with the spaciousness of the room, I felt, made a contribution to my thinking. I enjoyed the room and there was plenty of room for me to look around. When I was thinking I didn't focus my eyes; they just rested in different places. The real difference lay in what I was seeing inside my head.

Most buildings are not so beautiful but many have a view of nature to look at which can be helpful to the coaching relationship. There is something uplifting about looking at nature. Green grass, water (a river or pond) trees, sky, sun, clouds even rain – nature often engenders positive feelings in a person. When people look out at nature you can often see them take a deep breath and slightly relax their body. A lovely place provides something positive to look at and helps to expand the thinking. In your guidelines for clients ask them to find a place that they enjoy being in.

Somewhere with a variety of seating options

Before you first meet clients, you have no idea what their preference might be for seating. Chairs that are comfortable for some are not comfortable for others and you don't want any discomfort distracting them. If they are choosing the venue, you can trust that they will choose a place where they know they can sit comfortably. If you have to choose the venue, find one that offers a variety of seating choices so you can give clients the opportunity to choose seating that is preferable for them.

Room for movement

Sometimes when working with people it is useful to be able to move about. People experience the topic physically as well as mentally so it can be useful to explore the topic using a physical experience rather than just thinking about it.

I remember working with one client who said that she couldn't move forward with her plans. She couldn't even think about them. Something was stopping her. We had explored this by thinking, but she was stuck firmly. Thinking about it was not helping. So I asked where she felt the blockage and it was in her feet. So I encouraged her to explore this with movement. We both stood up and I asked her how far she could walk. She could step forward with one foot but not the other. I then asked her whether it was her whole foot and she realized she could lift her heel off the floor but not the ball of her foot. We finally established that she could drag the second foot across the floor to meet the first foot. This brought her to a metaphorical wall that she could look over and see what was on the other side. That was as far as she could go. I asked her what this meant in the context of the topic. She said that she now felt that she could have a look at what her options might be and give them some thought – a very different place to the one she was in 10 minutes before. The physical movement had translated into a change in thinking. Luckily we were in a private room with no possible observers. Had we been in a more public place she may have been reluctant to move about and the shift in her thinking may not have happened.

For this reason an ideal venue will offer the space to move about, perhaps one with a garden area or a part of the room that feels 'cordoned' off. If you are not familiar with the venue, when you arrive check whether there are places available that would afford space to move about should the need arise.

On the subject of movement, coaching while walking is becoming increasingly popular, and by its very nature meets many of the criteria listed above. The coaching relationship has a different feel to it when walking. The movement in walking seems to enhance the movement in the thinking. If you are walking find somewhere where there are seated alternatives available if clients arrive and decide they don't want to walk, for example if the weather is too inclement. Also it's handy to have somewhere to go for a coffee and reflect on the coaching experience at the end of the session.

Privacy and confidentiality

The key here is to find a place to work where the client will feel comfortable exploring any topic that may come up in the coaching. In the contracting you are likely to have raised the fact that sometimes the coaching can surface emotions that might be quite uncomfortable or that clients may want to explore topics that are private or highly confidential. Clients can judge where they can best explore these topics. Often the place they choose is not private, in fact a lot of coaching takes place in very public places, but it offers them a level of privacy that they are comfortable with. If you have to suggest a public space to work in, select a venue that is usually rarely frequented or offers areas that provide a good measure of privacy.

A change of environment

A change of venue is also worth considering periodically. We can be creatures of habit. You might meet your client in the same venue every time; in doing so you might notice that the client also settles into a habitual way of thinking. As the client arrives in the same place physically they may also do so mentally, for example if they have been working on a problem where they have felt stuck. A change of location might help to create a shift in the thinking.

Another reason for changing the venue is to support a change in the coaching relationship. Perhaps the learning needs to move to another level, or there is a change of topic, or the goals have changed – anything where a different venue might augment the change that is needed.

The change can be as simple as choosing new seats or altering the seating arrangement within the same location, or going for a walk while coaching rather than sitting in one place. If walking is already a regular feature in the coaching and something needs to shift in the client, creating some kind of variation in the route may help to facilitate the change, whether it's a new route, a new start or finish point, a completely new location, walking the same circuit but in the opposite direction or any other variation.

I was working with a client whose aim was to operate at a more strategic level in his current role. After a period of time he felt that he was achieving this and he was now ready to consider his next role. His new goal was to move into a higher level role. To support the change I proposed a change of venue for the coaching, together with my reasoning. We changed from using a meeting room close to his office to meeting in an external place. It's hard to measure what the difference was, but the change of venue appeared to support a change in his thinking. He arrived at the coaching differently to previous sessions. He was much more eager to talk about longer term future plans than what was happening previously.

Locating within the environment

The venue has been selected and you are meeting up for the session. I invite you to pay attention to where and how you locate yourself in the venue. How you sit (or walk together) can influence the relationship. How you position yourself in relation to the client will send a message to the client about your roles in this coaching relationship. You want it to indicate an equal and trusting relationship; you want clients to be in the place that best suits them and their learning while supporting the conscious choices you need to make. Below are the factors to consider.

Facilitating the client decision

When you arrive at the venue invite clients to choose a place to sit (or walk) where they can do their best thinking. If they have arrived before you and are already seated, don't assume that they have chosen the best place. Check with them before you get settled.

If you arrive at the venue before the clients, locate yourself quite close to the entrance. When they arrive gather your belongings, stand up and move forwards to greet them. Look around the room while inviting them to choose a place to work. You are making it clear that the choice is theirs and you are happy to move.

Choose your position in relation to the clients

Once they have decided where they want to sit, choose your position carefully. Here are some questions to ask yourself:

- Where can I place myself so that I can observe them closely without being in their direct line of sight?
- Where can I sit so that we are at eye level to each other?
- Where can I sit so that there is nothing to act as a barrier between us?

Line of sight

People will look almost anywhere but at the person they are talking to. So position yourself slightly to the side of them so that you are not blocking their view but where it will only take a small move of their head to look at you when they want to.

In contrast you want to be able to observe them quite closely. You don't need to look at the view – you want to be able to see their eyes, their face and their body language quite easily. So while you sit to one side of them, you face towards them. If you were both to look straight ahead, your own line of vision would end at the client, whereas you will not appear in their line of vision at all.

Eye level

You are both equal in this relationship so position yourself so that there is no suggestion of hierarchy. If sitting, try to make sure that your seats are at about the same height as each other, so your eyes are at about the same level.

Once I was coaching in a group setting, after asking the client where she wanted to work. I found myself standing and she was seated, with no available seats near her. I chose Evident Coach mode and explained that my standing up while she was sitting was uncomfortable for me and I wasn't sure how helpful it would be to the coaching. Even before I finished speaking she took on the responsibility of the decision. Rather than make room for me to sit down, as I anticipated, she chose to stand with me. Now we were at the same level. During the coaching we started meandering around the room exploring different aspects of the topic in different parts of the room.

No barriers

A table or a desk can sometimes feel like a barrier in the coaching relationship, particularly in the early stages. Sitting behind a desk (or something that resembles a desk) can also give an impression of hierarchy. To reinforce equality in the coaching relationship, try to locate yourself in relation to the client so that there are no physical barriers between you. This does not always suit the clients' preference: some people feel more comfortable on the other side of a desk or table. If this is the case find a way to diminish the potential barrier or hierarchy effect.

Check in with clients

Once you have located yourself do a final check with clients. How does it feel for them? Sometimes clients will choose to make some final adjustments,

I remember sitting down at the same side of a table with a client who promptly moved position so we were facing each other across the table. This presented two aspects that were unlikely to support the coaching: I was directly in her line of sight, and we had a potential barrier between us. After building rapport with her I turned slightly as if to look out of the window, resting my arm on the table as if it were the arm of my chair. She turned and did the same. Perhaps it was just me (recognizing that this might be more to do with me than the client) but the session felt more relaxed for both of us after this change in position.

for example moving slightly closer or further away or changing the angle at which they are sitting.

Sometimes clients' choice of location in the venue may surprise you but invariably it will be the right place for them. Often people choose to sit with their back to a wall and/or facing a window. However, I remember being really surprised when someone I worked with sat with their back to the window facing a wall. I had worked with her a few times and she had never sat in this way before. On the wall was a large mural. As the session progressed she used the mural as a metaphor for the topic we were exploring that day. I would not have chosen that position, but the mural was really helpful.

Self-preparation

Here I offer you a routine to help you to achieve your best coaching presence as described in the Introduction. You start and finish the preparation by being quiet and still. It is when you have a quiet and still mind that your inner wisdom will come through. Learn and follow this process until you no longer have to follow it. Just being quiet and still and deciding to focus on the client becomes enough. The aim of the preparation is to bring the client to the forefront of your attention and to get you into the best place mentally for the coaching. It can be broken down into the following key elements:

- Park your own mental clutter (Whitworth *et al*, 2009).
- Focus your attention towards the client and his or her needs.
- Be calm and relaxed.
- Decide how you want to 'be' with this client.

Benefits of regularly preparing for your coaching in this way include:

- Reducing the amount of time it takes to achieve your coaching presence.

- Increasing your capacity to identify and assess options in the moment.

- Increasing your capacity to be creative, responsive and adaptive to the client's needs.

- Increasing your ability to register any changes in physicality, feelings or emotions you experience in the coaching and make it easier to recognize whether it is useful data for the coaching (see Chapter 4).

Preparation routine

1 Start by breathing slowly and deeply and maintain this slow and deep breathing throughout the whole routine (see Mindfulness and meditation in Chapter 8).

2 Focus on you. Check out how you are feeling. What is your underlying mood? Do you have any aches and pains? Register and acknowledge these feelings. Examples might include feeling stressed due to issues at home, having a headache or back pain, or being tired because you didn't sleep well last night.

3 Consider things that may be playing on your mind. Make a choice to let these go. If there are things you need to do later find a way to park these so that you will remember them, for instance making a written or mental note.

4 Decide to focus on the client.

5 Read any notes you have made about previous sessions with this client and remind yourself what is or was going on for him or her. Remind yourself of any specific goals the client may have that he or she is working on in coaching.

6 If the client has sent you reflective notes, read them. Make a note of any questions that he or she has raised for themselves, or that he or she would like to be asked at the next session. I will sometimes write these questions down: it cements them in my mind and I can

refer to the note easily in the session if I need to remember the questions correctly.

7 Picture the clients (spend some time doing this). Remind yourself where you met last time, where they sat, how they sat, how they were dressed. Also recall where they work, who they work with, what their background is, what you know about their learning preferences. Also recall what you know about what is going on in their lives, personally and professionally.

8 Read your reflective notes from the previous session (discussed in Chapter 8). Spend some time considering any resolutions you made about how you might want to work differently with this client. Imagine yourself working with the client in this new way.

9 Reflect on your supervision sessions (also discussed in Chapter 8). You may have discussed this client with your supervisor, or discussed a topic that may have some relevance to this client. Read any notes you have made or reflect on the learning from the supervision. What does it mean for your work with this client? Imagine yourself working with this client when you have taken account of your learning.

10 Consider the environment you are going to be working in with the client. Thinking about the factors discussed earlier, are there any adjustments that could make the most of the environment?

11 Now put everything down. Relax and allow all the conscious thinking to fade into your unconscious. Remember to breathe slowly and deeply. Focus on the world around you. Take a few relaxed moments to enjoy and appreciate nature; focus on trees, greenery, flowers, water, sky, clouds – whatever you can see.

Preparation constraints

'Oh yes,' I hear you say, 'just when do I have time to do all that!' Often the reality is that we don't have a great deal of time to spend on our preparation. It helps if you allow time in between sessions so that you can refocus, but often demands mean that this time is limited. But the routine can be flexed. It can be done in stages and the order can be varied. If you have a busy day ahead you can do steps 4–10 the night before and 1–3 first thing in the morning. Then all you need to do between sessions is a scan of your notes and steps 4 and 11. If nothing else I recommend that you always take time for these two steps in between sessions, even with 'spur of the minute' coaching. Decide to focus on the client, and take some deep breaths to help you to relax and focus.

What I find helpful (when I do it) is meditation. When I do this in the morning it really sets me up for the day. Unfortunately our clients don't often arrive in a good state for the coaching session. When the client arrives in a busy frame of mind it would be quite natural for you to start feeling the same way (Goleman, 2007; see also 'contagious emotions' in Chapter 2). When others are feeling agitated, emotional or stressed it's easy for us to hook into the same feeling. You can often see this affecting teams: one person arrives in a bad mood and within minutes the whole team feels the same. This is where your own preparation is helpful. When the client arrives, hold onto the calm state that you have achieved through your preparation. By doing this any transfer of feelings taking place will be from you to the client and he or she will start to 'catch' your calm and relaxed state. You might have to adapt your approach later, but holding onto this at the outset helps you to maintain your presence.

Facilitating client presence

When clients arrive with their own mental clutter (Whitworth et al, 2009) it will be hard for them to access their inner wisdom. This wisdom will not surface until they have a quiet and still mind. You help them to achieve this. It's possible that some of the clutter they bring with them is related to the topic for coaching. Helping them to be ready for the coaching will include helping them to identify what is relevant and to park whatever is not.

To help the client to get into a quiet and still frame of mind you can follow the process outlined below. Some of the stages are simultaneous and there are similarities to your own preparation. You will take steps to prepare clients regardless of how they arrive for coaching; the difference will be in how long it takes and which modes of presence you might have to use to get them ready. You might be surprised to find that you often use all four modes in this process. Here are some tips for helping clients to prepare for coaching:

- Pay immediate attention.
- Create a shift using physicality.
- Identify and let go of potential distractions.
- Slow breathing exercise.

Pay immediate attention

Pay attention to clients from the moment you greet them; the case study below highlights the importance of this. Their body language, vocal tone and pace, eye movements, their breathing and language will give you indications about how much clutter they have brought with them and how ready they are to start coaching. Pay attention to how they are today and notice how this compares to previous sessions. You are looking for signs that there

During a workshop one of my coaching sessions was video recorded. The camcorder was recording while we both got ready for the session. My client was a happy and bubbly character, so smiling and happy we started the coaching session. We only had 20 minutes for the session. I'd been with the group (which included the client) for a couple of days already, so I did not worry about preparing her for the session. We agreed the topic and got started. Shortly into the session she changed the subject. She started talking about something that was bothering her from earlier in the day. The issue was discussed then we got back to the coaching topic, but the flow had been interrupted.

But here's the key point of this case study: later I watched the video recording. What I saw was startling! In the few minutes that I was taking to prepare myself, my client's body language and facial expression made it very clear that there was something bothering her. Her body was slumped, her head hung down, suggesting there was something weighing her down. As soon as she realized we were ready to start, her whole demeanour changed: she straightened up and her face beamed. I thought that I was pretty good at paying attention to my client but I completely missed this through concentrating on my own needs at the outset. Despite her attempt to hide the issue it came back in the session. If I had taken the time to prepare her this would have been surfaced and dealt with before the coaching got started.

may be something to distract them from the coaching today. Your aim in helping them to prepare for the coaching is to minimize the chance of this happening.

Create a shift using physicality

Once you have sat down together (or are getting ready to start your walk) notice how clients are seated, how they position themselves, how they hold their body, their posture, what they are doing with their arms and legs. Does all this indicate someone who is calm and alert and ready to focus on the coaching topic? If not, using your own physicality can help to facilitate a change in the client to a relaxed and alert state that is more conducive to learning. You choose to position your body in a way that mirrors the client: if he or she is sat on the edge of the seat, do the same. Do this for a minute or two. When you feel ready change your posture to something that is more relaxed and alert. I find that when I feel ready to change posture it is a good indicator that the client may be ready too. When in rapport you change position, and he or she will usually follow; you can use this knowingly to help the client to be ready for the coaching.

Identify and let go of potential distractions

First, focus the client's attention on the potential distractions so that later attention can be diverted away from them, at least for long enough to be able to coach without them resurfacing. Encourage clients to talk about key things that are on their mind without probing into any detail. The aim at

I was coaching someone who started off sitting with her legs crossed, both hands clasped firmly around one knee. Her body was bolt upright and arms locked into position. Her breathing was fast and shallow, her words sounded clipped. I mirrored her position. I crossed my legs, sat upright, clasped my hands around my knee and held that position. After a short while I chose to shift position. I took a deep breath, let go of my knee and sat back in my chair and shifted to a more comfortable position. In the same instant she let go of her leg and started gesticulating with her hands, her body relaxed, her breathing changed and the words seemed to flow more easily.

this point is just to identify potential distractions. While they are talking you will probably hear plenty of topics that could be explored through the coaching, but don't follow up on them yet. Remember what they talk about as it may become relevant later.

Once clients have talked about the key things, ask if anything they have mentioned relates to the coaching topic. Park this for now then ask them to find a way of letting go of the other things they have mentioned so that they will remember what they need to later. Often they don't need to do any-thing: talking about them has been enough; at other times they might need to make a note so they don't forget. Once they have done what they need to, ask them if they are ready to start the coaching. You are giving a clear indi-cation that the coaching is about to start and it's time to let those potential distractions go.

Slow breathing exercise

For some people who are quite agitated or stressed the process above is not enough to help them to be ready to focus attention on the coaching. A few minutes of slow and deep breathing can help to settle them down and let go of some of the stress that they have arrived with. Sometimes an offer of a few minutes of silence and deep breathing is welcomed to help them to regain their composure.

Signs that they are ready for coaching

If you have gone through the above process, clients will tell you that they are ready for the coaching. In addition you will observe some physical signs: they appear to be settled, relaxed but alert. Their eyes are focused on you rather than looking around the room. Often they have stopped talking and are looking at you as if to say, 'Now what?'

Interrupt the process

Often the above process will only take a few minutes but there are times when this preparation can get protracted, for example the client may be delaying getting started. In Visible Coach mode (Chapter 6) I talk about using interruption as an intervention. While you want to surface potential distractions, the preparation itself may be acting as a distraction; here's an example.

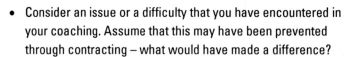

As part of the preparation, one client liked to take time to reflect on how the coaching had impacted on his work. In fact in the latest session we spent very little time on the coaching as the session got curtailed. In my reflective practice I noticed that in the last two sessions this period of reflection had become extended. Next time we met I chose to interrupt his process. He started to reflect as he was in the habit of doing but rather than letting him continue, I interrupted and brought to his attention how long we had spent previously in reflection and I asked him what he thought about this. It turned out that he was approaching a crossroads in his career and he was putting off thinking about it. We then used the session to explore this as the topic.

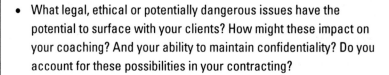

Reflective questions

Contracting

- Consider an issue or a difficulty that you have encountered in your coaching. Assume that this may have been prevented through contracting – what would have made a difference?

- What legal, ethical or potentially dangerous issues have the potential to surface with your clients? How might these impact on your coaching? And your ability to maintain confidentiality? Do you account for these possibilities in your contracting?

- What might you do differently in your contracting?

Environment

- How do you decide the venue for any coaching sessions?

- How might your current choice of venue be impacting on your coaching relationships?

- How often do you change venue or location with your clients? Consider one of your current clients. How might a change of venue impact on this client?

- What do you consider before locating yourself in relation to your client?

Self-preparation

- How do you prepare yourself for your coaching sessions?

- How has reading this section changed your thinking about your preparation?

- What aspects do you want to build into your preparation?

Client presence

- How do you help your clients prepare for the coaching session?

- How has reading this section changed your thinking about how you help your client's presence?

What's impacting on your coaching?

02

In this chapter I invite you to consider the factors that may be showing up in your coaching but outside of your awareness. Think about the factors that have influenced the person that you are today – genes, upbringing, education, life experiences. The things that have shaped who we are will also be present in our coaching.

Our brain has taken on board a lifetime of learning and experiences and is using this to inform and shape our thinking, feeling and behaving. This does not stop when we start coaching so it must be influencing our coaching. It's not good or bad, right or wrong, it just is. Sometimes it will benefit our clients; sometimes it may limit the benefit of the coaching for the client. When coaching we need to take notice of what is influencing the way we think feel or behave; fortunately we have lots of information available to help us to work it out.

Since before Socrates was alive humans have been trying to make sense of how the mind works. Many psychological theories and models, psychometric tools, self-perception inventories and questionnaires have been developed to help us try to understand ourselves and others better. When used in the right way these tools can be used to gain insights about ourselves and provide a way of helping us to appreciate the diversity between ourselves and other people. They provide a lens through which we can view ourselves and a language that can be used as a basis for reflective practice to learn and understand ourselves better. We can use these lenses to increase our own self-awareness, develop our skills and learn to self-regulate.

Self-awareness

At this juncture I think it is appropriate to explain what I mean by 'self-awareness'. When you are self-aware you can articulate a wide range of knowledge about yourself, including your values, beliefs, attitudes, preferences, assumptions, personality and what may be informing your thinking, feelings, emotions and behaviours. You understand something about how your upbringing impacts and influences you as an adult. You know what triggers your emotional responses. You know your strengths and current limitations, and you know how you want to develop yourself further. You have a strong sense of your own identity and you understand, appreciate and can articulate the diversity between yourself and others. You are aware of how you are different in a variety of contexts and you are aware of your impact on others.

What you do with this awareness is key. Armed with this knowledge and understanding you moderate and regulate yourself. You choose new ways of thinking and behaving to counteract some of the influences. You notice your own physical and emotional responses in time to choose whether to respond differently if appropriate. You notice how others respond to you and you adapt your behaviour accordingly. You are able to convert your internal dialogue to something that may be more helpful and positive. Finally you have a strong idea about who you are when you are your 'best self' and you strive to achieve this.

As you develop your self-awareness and self-regulation you are better equipped to filter out your own personal influences to help clients with their own thinking. How do you develop this self-awareness? The answer lies in using multiple channels of perception yourself, to reflect on what you think, feel, and how you behave. Reflective practice (see Chapter 8) can play an important part in developing this self-awareness. What follows are some aspects for you to consider. At the end of the book you will find references and further reading suggestions on some of the tools, theories and models mentioned.

Personality

There are a wide variety of diagnostic tools available that are designed to help us to identify aspects of how our minds work, our personality type or traits, our preferences, our predispositions, our learning style, our stage of development. Examples of these include Myers-Briggs Type Indicator

(MBTI) (Briggs Myers and Myers, 1980), Belbin's team role theory, Honey and Mumford's (1986) learning styles and Torbert's seven transformations of leadership (Rooke and Torbert, 2011). These attempt to define aspects of behaviour or how we might take in and use information. They offer a view based on self-perception of data collected on a specific date and time. Some argue that the results would be the same every time, others that the aspects assessed might be variable and contextual.

Whatever you may think of them, they offer the opportunity to view ourselves from different perspectives. They can help to open our minds to analyse ourselves and see how others might view us. They can also help us to articulate the differences between ourselves and others. When we assess the information provided in these diagnostic tools, regardless of whether we agree with the output, we can learn something about how our own minds tick, and how and why we act in certain ways in certain contexts, resulting in a realization of what might be influencing our coaching. Until we focus attention on how our personality, preferences, styles, etc are influencing our coaching practice they will continue to influence.

Throughout my career I have completed many diagnostic tools and learnt a lot about myself, but it was years before I made the connection between these and my coaching. I needed to review what I had learnt through these tools specifically in the context of my coaching. If you have not done this take another look at what you have learnt and identify some characteristics that you know about yourself. Then for each characteristic consider how this might be influencing your coaching in theory. Then start to notice it in your coaching and reflect on it and find out how it actually impacts.

Below are just a few examples of how aspects of personality traits, types or preferences may influence your coaching. I offer these as a starting point to get you thinking about this; there will be so much more. I am purposely avoiding labels as it is the influence in the coaching that is important. I also want to make it clear that when talking about influence there is no negative or positive judgement and the outcome can vary from client to client.

- If you prefer to take a well-planned, disciplined approach to things, you may adopt a similar approach in your coaching. This may show up by always using a specific structure to guide your client through the exploration.

- If you have a preference for spontaneity and flexibility you may prefer to have no structure in your coaching.

- If you need to understand how everything fits together, and all the whys and wherefores of a job before you do it, you may spend a lot of time in the coaching helping the client to work out and understand all the connections in a particular situation.

- If you like to take time to consider things from every angle and perspective before drawing any conclusions, it is likely that you will encourage the client to do this in the coaching.

- If you tend to think as you speak, rather than before you speak, you may start an intervention and change your mind as you work through it.

- If you don't like 'waffle' or become easily bored by the minutiae you may encourage your clients to skip through this so that they get to the point quicker in their exploration.

- If you prefer to think things through in a logical way, you may avoid helping your client to explore feelings, or vice versa.

- What is your approach to risk? If you like to take chances you may encourage your clients to do the same. If you are more cautious this may cause you to steer your clients towards safer options.

- If you love new ideas and trying out new things you may steer your client towards new ideas rather than the tried and trusted.

- How are you with managing time? Do your coaching sessions always finish on time? Or do they often overrun?

Do any of these resonate with you? Think about how you want to be different. What will help you to achieve that? Bear in mind that anything you may decide you want to change could take time and effort. Some of these behaviours and ways of thinking have been with you for most of your life. With attention and perseverance you can choose to think and behave in different ways for the benefit of the client. Here's an example of a change of my own.

Through feedback gained from a diagnostic tool I realized that I have a preference for thinking as I speak. I often don't know what I am going to say until I say it. As I speak I find that I can disagree with myself as soon as I hear what I've said! At the time I assumed that there was nothing I could do about this. I thought that the diagnostic tool was telling me that this is how my brain is wired. I used the information to acknowledge that others might be different and sometimes I needed to allow other people time to think before they spoke.

Later I realized that in my coaching, this thinking as I speak was not always serving me well, and I resolved to change. In my reflective practice (see Chapter 8) I realized that often I would be happy with my interventions but sometimes I wish I had chosen something else. On reflection I could see alternative interventions that I had not considered in the moment and which perhaps may have been more beneficial for the client. My predisposition to think as I speak caused me to use the first intervention that came to mind and I would not consider other options that might be appropriate.

I resolved to think about options before deciding upon single coaching interventions. I had to learn to take time to think before choosing. But it didn't just happen – deciding to do it was one thing; actually doing it something else! I had to work at it. I used my reflective practice to identify times when there were other options available that I had not considered in the moment. I kept on reflecting on this in hindsight until eventually I started to notice other options in the moment. Over time I became more adept at considering other options in the moment. It took a while but eventually my brain learnt how to reflect in the moment and took on board this way of working. (For more, see Schön, 1991, on the 'reflective practitioner'.)

Nurture or nature?

Here's an age-old question! Are we the way we are because of nature or nurture? From the information we have available at the moment, and from what I have learnt about myself, I would say that it's both. My upbringing has certainly informed my thinking and behaviour. This is another useful lens through which to view and understand ourselves and to consider what might be impacting on our coaching.

Some schools of thought show that we can track some of the ways we think and behave right back to what we learnt in our early childhood. They provide models and theories that can be used to help us to think through how we are still holding on to ways of thinking and behaving that stem from this time. Much of what we learnt in our early years has stood us in good stead, but some ways of thinking and behaving may not be serving us so well now.

In your development so far you may have already learnt how your upbringing might be influencing you. Think about this now in the context of your coaching practice. Again without using labels, here are some ways in which patterns of thinking and behaviour might show up in your coaching. Some of these you might argue are nothing to do with how you are brought up, but I offer these as a lens through which to view your behaviour rather than an actual fact.

- How does your internal dialogue impact on your coaching? Maybe you said something, or used an intervention that didn't go as well as you would have liked. You berate yourself for getting it wrong and tell yourself you must try harder to get it right next time. You start thinking about all the things that you could have said or done. The most obvious impact is that while all this is going on you miss a whole section of the client's exploration. But how does the way you respond to yourself when you get things 'wrong' impact on how you respond to the client when they get things 'wrong'?

- Are you constantly in a rush, running out of time and needing to get things done quickly, often feeling a need to hurry people up? This might impact in your coaching by pushing the client to get through the exploration very quickly. Here is another of my examples.

- When people find themselves in a difficult situation is it your first instinct to rescue them? When someone starts crying do you feel the need to help them to stop? Is your instinctive reaction, 'Please don't cry'? In coaching there may be some significant learning from a situation that clients find difficult or upsetting. If you feel the need to rescue them rather than explore the situation they may miss out on this learning.

- As a child did you get the impression that your achievements were never enough? As soon as one goal was achieved you had to look to the next one. How much do you celebrate your successes now in adulthood? If you are someone who doesn't celebrate success (a common British trait), then you are probably not paying this any attention in your coaching. You may not be recognizing, or helping your clients to recognize their successes.

- Are you a peacekeeper, someone who doesn't like conflict and wants everyone to be happy? If this is the case you may be reluctant to provide any significant challenge to your clients' thinking. You back down rather than say something that they might not like.

- Do you find that there are some people you feel uncomfortable with for no apparent reason? Some clients will trigger old memories – your mind (acting in your interest and outside of your awareness) will respond in the way that it learnt to respond to the old memory. This will influence how you react with the client in the moment.

I was one of those people who is always in a rush. Let's not mess about, let's just get to the point. Here is how it manifested itself in my coaching practice.

With new clients I would take a short amount of time in the first session to agree a goal for the programme. I would quickly grasp a basic understanding of their goal and then I would progress the coaching. But I noticed a pattern emerging. A few sessions into the coaching programme clients would realize that their original goal was not what they wanted at all, and we would have to revisit the goal for the programme. In my rush to get to the coaching I cut short the initial exploration of the goal, and this resulted in a slowing down of the coaching process. I have since found that taking time over exploring and clarifying the goal can save a lot of time later! The amount of time spent varies from client to client but they always report that this exploration of the goal provides significant benefits in itself.

I started to recognize how my upbringing influenced the person I am now through a period of counselling. My understanding deepened and developed through reflection using the lens of aspects of transactional analysis (Stewart and Joines, 1987). In particular, learning about ego states helped me to handle my internal dialogue.

Life experience

So far I have touched on how nature (personality) and nurture (upbringing) may impact on our coaching. Now I talk about how our life experiences can impact.

These next factors – values, beliefs, assumptions, judgements and solutions – all show up in our coaching practice but originate from our life experience. Some may be easy to spot but many are so deeply ingrained that it is very hard to recognize when it is happening. It is unlikely that a diagnostic tool will bring these to the surface; rather you have to go looking for them to become aware of them. You need to make a conscious effort to consider these, and this is often easier with some outside help. Some can be surfaced through reflective practice, others may be more easily identified through coaching, supervision or feedback from others.

Values

Our values are to do with what's important to us in our life and work, and what we believe to be right or wrong. They are the rules that we live our lives by or what we feel is important to have in our lives. We form many of our values early on in childhood and for many they remain throughout adulthood. They inform the choices we make, our beliefs and assumptions and the judgements we make about ourselves and others. We don't realize we are doing it but we expect others to conform to our values and are surprised when they don't. When we get angry at the actions or words of others it is often because they have infringed one of our values. Our values are one of the myriad of things that our brain has assimilated into our automatic thinking and processing, so often it takes some digging before we can articulate these fully. We know some of them at a superficial level, but the real values are found when we explore deeper, below our own level two awareness (discussed in the Introduction).

Beliefs

My definition of a belief is something that is thought to be true based on our experience of the world. It can be informed by past experiences and what has been learnt as a result of gaining certain outcomes. It can relate to what we think about ourselves or situations or what might happen given a set of circumstances, and this affects our actions in those contexts. When we believe something to be true we may expect others to think and feel the same, or we might expect them to have the same experience as us.

What we believe will affect what we do or say, the rights that we give ourselves and our outcomes. I'm not sure where this originated but I first came across this idea in a book by Back and Back (2005). It is a cycle, so the outcomes either reinforce the belief or generate a new belief which then result in different behaviours (which in turn results in different outcomes, and so it goes on).

I think it will be easier to demonstrate how beliefs might impact on your coaching by providing a personal example. This is how a belief about myself has changed and how it impacted on my coaching both before and after the change.

One day I attended a workshop, part of which focused on using your intuition when coaching. This brought to my attention that this was missing in my coaching. Up to this point this was outside of my awareness. Somewhere along the line I had stopped using my intuition when coaching. I realized that the reason for this was that I believed that my intuition was not trustworthy. How did I come to that conclusion? In the past I would say things based on my intuition and I would often get it wrong. My clients would deny or rail against the intervention. This reinforced my belief that I could not trust it. In reality it did not happen every time, but enough times for me to doubt myself.

This decision to stop using my intuition was not a conscious one. Here is what I think are the stages that I went through before this happened, all of them outside of my awareness:

1 I used my intuition with someone and they rejected this.

2 I made a judgement and concluded that I had got it wrong.

3 This went against my value of always having to do things right.

4 I noticed each time I used my intuition and got it 'wrong'.

5 I ignored or discounted any other explanation for what had happened.

6 I ignored or discounted all the times when I got it 'right'.

7 I assumed that it had to be something I had done wrong.

8 I concluded that my intuition was not trustworthy.

9 I decided that I should no longer use my intuition and withdrew my right to use it in my coaching.

The course provided me with an opportunity to reassess my belief. As you may have registered from my guiding beliefs, I have now come to the conclusion that my intuition can be trustworthy, and it's ok to get it wrong sometimes. I learnt that when I use my intuition in a slightly different way I am more often right than I am wrong. I consciously reinstated the right to use my intuition in my coaching. As a result clients have been able to explore their topics through a perspective that they didn't get from me before and this has provided them with some great insights.

I didn't wake up one day and decide that I wasn't going to use my intuition any more. This example demonstrates how the brain takes some learning into its automatic processing outside of your awareness. I can recognize now that points 3 and 7 were very much influenced by my upbringing. Point 3 was a value I had learnt very early in life that no longer served me well. Point 7 was a learnt behaviour. Point 8 became a belief based on my experience and the (somewhat distorted) evidence that informed this.

When you break down the sequence of events as I have done here you can see how your values and beliefs can inform your current thinking, feeling and behaviour and you can probably work out how these have come into being. In this example there was a long-standing value, a long-standing belief, and another belief that had been based on and reinforced by my adult experiences. I also mention judgements and assumptions, which I move on to discuss now.

Assumptions

In the above example I had evidence (albeit flawed) to support the belief about my intuition. An assumption is when we think something without any proof to substantiate the thinking. Point 7 above is a good example of where there was no proof to substantiate the assumption that had informed my thinking, feeling or behaviour for a big chunk of my life. When something went wrong, I assumed it must be my fault therefore I needed to work out how to adapt my behaviour. Sometimes it is my fault, and I do need to adapt my behaviour, but sometimes it's not. I've learnt that when I use my intuition in a coaching session, the denial response from the client may be due to the fact that he or she is not comfortable with discussing this aspect and it's easier to deny it than to agree and have to face talking about it. The assumption that it must be me getting it wrong let the client off the hook of exploring the aspect and potentially meant that he or she missed out on some profound learning.

Quite often we are provided with information by the sponsor about our clients before we meet them. It's human nature to make assumptions about the client based on this information, so be careful about how much you discuss the client with the sponsor before meeting them. Even with no prior information we can make assumptions about people just by looking at them.

Some assumptions are very easy to spot, and luckily had not adversely influenced any of my conversations with her before I realized. But other assumptions, like the one mentioned above, are not so easy to spot. Often others can notice them in you quite easily (in the same way that you can probably notice them in others), but you don't notice them in yourself without an intervention.

I had just started working with a new client. We were clarifying goals and as we were doing this she stated that she was going to reduce the number of hours she was working. She regularly worked seven or eight hours over the weekends and worked late every night. She was going to stop working weekends. I helped her to explore the current situation with a view to helping her to work out how she was going to be able to achieve this. No matter which way we looked at it the answer was simple for her: she was just going to stop taking work home at the weekends. Her perception was that this was easy. I wasn't so sure but my interventions were getting nowhere so I moved on with the coaching. At the end of the session her feedback was very positive and she was really pleased with the insights and learning experience.

Despite the positive feedback, I discussed this with my supervisor. I felt slightly unsettled by the session but couldn't pinpoint why. Through my supervision I realized that an assumption had informed my coaching: I was assuming that she would find it difficult to stop taking work home at the weekends. Several years ago I decided to reduce the number of hours I was working by a day a week and I found it hard to do. It involved quite a bit of planning, changes to the way I prioritized my work and training others to take on more. I assumed that it would be quite difficult for her to do because it was for me. This assumption was informing my interventions, which were aimed at getting her to appreciate how hard it would be to achieve and to plan how she would do it.

Next time we met, she had stopped working at home at the weekends. All she had needed was to acknowledge that it was happening and that it was going against her values doing it. She had realized that she was not being a good role model for her daughter – it was important for her to see her mum taking time off at the weekends. This was enough for her to stop doing it!

As I mentioned at the beginning of the chapter, sometimes the influences will be positive, other times not so. The issue isn't whether it was right or wrong, positive or negative, but that there was an influence, based on an assumption, that was outside of my awareness and this drove my line of questioning. Quite possibly it was the extended exploration that helped her to recognize these things. Luckily in this case it appeared to be helpful.

Judgements

What makes something a judgement is the element of evaluation or assessment. Judgements are linked to values, beliefs and sometimes assumptions. You have to believe something in order to make a judgement. If someone were to ask me to judge how good a computer game is I would find it difficult to do immediately because I don't know much about them. To make the judgement I would have to come up with some beliefs about what makes a good computer game. Show me a computer game that is based on violence and murder and I will immediately judge that it is not a good game, because I already have the belief that this kind of violent stimulus reduces people's empathy for others, and I have a value that says empathy is a good thing.

We make judgements all the time. It's a fundamental part of the decision-making process and our days are filled with having to make decisions. In coaching we have to decide which interventions to use and this will be based on an assessment of what we see, hear and feel, and what we know about how our interventions might be able to help. So judgements will always influence our coaching. Where judgement may not be so helpful in the coaching relationship is when we find ourselves making an evaluation of something the client is saying, or something about his or her behaviour. Is something good or bad, right or wrong, strong or weak, and so on?

I was working with a group that included one person who I felt very nervous around. I found it difficult to relax in her presence, and was constantly managing my responses to her. She laughed and smiled a lot and other people around her did not appear as uncomfortable as I felt. I couldn't see what the problem was. I thought perhaps she reminded me of someone (as discussed earlier) but I couldn't think who this might be. I thought my feelings would settle down but after two meetings this wasn't happening so I discussed the issue with my supervisor. Through this I learnt that the following had happened outside of my awareness:

1 Before meeting the group I had made an assumption that all the members would be experienced coaches.

2 When we were invited to provide feedback to each other I automatically expected a certain standard (a value) that this feedback should adhere to.

3 I assumed that experienced coaches would be able to meet this standard. She was completely unaware of this expectation.

4 Based on this standard I made a judgement about the quality of the feedback that she gave to me. Her feedback was valid. I judged that it had been delivered clumsily and that she could have done it more professionally. That judgement translated into a feeling about her as a person.

5 I discounted the fact that I consider myself to be an experienced coach who can sometimes be quite awkward and clumsy when giving feedback.

Going through the reflective process with my supervisor helped me to recognize first of all the assumption I had made, and then the unfairness of my expectation and judgement. I was able to realign my thinking based on the reality of the situation and as a result I was able to relax and work more effectively with her.

This is an example of something outside of my awareness influencing my work with the group and was definitely not helpful. I wonder what judgement you might be making of me, now that I have made this disclosure. Does it diminish the value you place on this book because you assume that I as the author should not be making judgements or assumptions like this? Does it make you question my ability? Because I'm human, I'm wondering whether I should be sharing this particular example. Do I assume that you will judge me and find me lacking and take it out of the book? Or do I assume that you will read it and accept it for what it is? An example of how any of us can get caught out by the assumptions and judgements that happen outside of our awareness.

A time when you might find yourself making judgements is when your client is generating ideas. You can almost hear yourself assessing each idea as it is mentioned. 'Oh yes, that's a good idea' or, 'Oh no, I don't think that will work' or, 'Oh yes – now you've got it – that's the one.' You might not tell the client what you are thinking but then the judgement might still inform your next intervention. Perhaps you steer the client to explore further the idea that you thought was best. Or you might encourage the client to explore one or two of the ideas, whilst ignoring those that you judged were inappropriate. If you are going to ensure that you are not allowing your judgement to inform your coaching you encourage the client to decide for him or herself which ideas to discard and which to explore further.

Remember also that there may be times when judgements are to be encouraged. I'm thinking about times when ethical, dangerous or legal issues arise, or perhaps there is evidence of mental health issues. In these scenarios you are not making a judgement about the client, but about the behaviours being demonstrated or discussed. Your judgement may inform an intervention to help the client to fully explore the consequences of any action being considered, or to seek further help.

Solutions

Often part of the reason we are selected as a coach is because we have a similar background to the clients we are working with. Sponsors often feel that the coaching will be of more value if the coach understands the work of the client. What this means is that you can often have ideas about potential solutions and these can influence your interventions.

Here's a dilemma for you to consider. You have encouraged the client to brainstorm some options for potential actions. You know a really good solution but no matter how much you encourage him or her to come up with more options, he or she has not mentioned it. What do you do? If you don't share it he or she might be missing out on a perfectly good solution, but how does telling him or her your idea gel with coaching or your contract?

In my work with developing coaches this is one of the most observable factors influencing coaching intervention. They have a potential solution in mind and it comes across in the question. It sounds like an open question but actually it is a disguised suggestion. The following are examples asked in coaching sessions where there has been no mention of this as a possible option prior to the question being asked:

- 'What do you think about talking to Fred about this issue?' Suggestion: Talk to Fred about the issue.

- 'What additional preparation do you think you should do before you see Jenny again?' Suggestion: You need to do more preparation.

- 'How do you feel about doing a survey to find out?' Suggestion: Do a survey.

- Often the question is even more obvious: 'Have you thought about doing…?' or 'Why don't you try…?'

This is a dilemma that I have faced regularly in my coaching. Sometimes I have offered the idea, sometimes not. I was determined not to tell my clients what to do but knowing that there was still one more idea to surface influenced my coaching interventions and I would encourage them to keep on searching for more options until they came up with my idea! The benefit of this is that as a result I became more adept and creative at helping my clients to brainstorm. My clients have benefitted because invariably they come up with a much wider range of potential options to choose from (compared to what they used to come up with) and often the latter ideas are the best ones. They don't need me to offer an idea, because they come up with so many good ideas for themselves. Whenever I offered the idea, they invariably disregarded it anyway!

Other factors

Contagious emotions

Emotions like anger, fear, sadness, joy and variations of these, are all emotions that appear to be highly contagious. If we are not careful we can 'catch' the emotions of others (Goleman, 2007). I touched on this in Chapter 1 when I talked about helping the client to prepare for the coaching. We usually have empathy for our clients and that might make us susceptible to 'catching' their emotions. If someone arrives at the coaching session feeling quite depressed today you may suddenly find that you feel it too. Continuing this example, if you feel depressed it reduces your capacity to think and be creative and can impact on the success of the coaching. Be careful to hold onto your own emotional state by preparing for the session, as outlined in Chapter 1.

Hooks

When working with our clients we can find that the topic under exploration is one that we ourselves might be wrangling with. We are constantly learning and developing, we have our own interpersonal issues, or development plans, or business issues. When listening to our clients we are looking out for indicators of what might be important for them, and we notice emphasis placed on particular words, phrases or topics. There is something about how they stress certain words or sentences that makes us think that this is something that needs exploring. However, sometimes the emphasis that we notice comes from how these words, sentences or topics resonate with us.

When we are working through a particular topic, or have a particular difficulty ourselves, we notice it more in others. Think about the last time you bought a new model of car. Before you bought the car I hazard a guess that you never saw one on the road; now that you own one, you spot hundreds of them. You have a heightened awareness for those particular cars. The same can be said of any topics or issues that you might have: you notice it more when other people mention the same topic or issue.

I was reconsidering the direction of my business. A few new options were opening up for me and I was starting to think about where and how I wanted to take my business forward. The same topic came up when coaching two of my clients. Both decided that the topic they wanted to explore was whether they wanted to do something different with their business. Was it a coincidence, or was it that my heightened awareness caused me to steer the coaching in that particular direction? In both cases I recognized this as a possibility and raised it with the clients to check that exploration of this topic was their first priority for the session.

Distractions

When working with people who are brand new to coaching I invite them to practise listening to another person for five minutes. Often people stop after just two or three minutes – they find it really hard to just keep on listening. We then analyse what was happening while they were listening and there are usually two dominant factors that get in the way. The first is the desire to add their own views about the topic and the second are the distractions that drag their attention away from the topic.

I could produce an almost endless list of the types of things that cause people to be distracted but here are just a few common examples:

- sights, sounds and smells that catch the attention;
- thinking about what they are going to have for tea;
- thinking about people or places that have been mentioned;
- considering what they would do if they were in the other person's place;
- remembering jobs that they need to do;
- thinking about things that happened at the weekend, or this morning, or what's happening this evening or weekend;
- reliving an argument they had with the children or partner this morning;
- noticing what someone else is doing in another room;
- wanting to listen into someone else's conversation instead.

Experienced coaches can find that these types of things pop into their minds while coaching. Everyone is susceptible to distractions. The trick is to notice it immediately and decide to let the thoughts go, rather than follow them through.

Soon after I got married a client mentioned someone called Ashley, which happens to be the name of my new husband. Immediately I was transported back to my wedding day. Much as I would have loved to spend a few minutes reminiscing about the day, I had to let it go immediately so that I could continue to focus on my client.

Levels of awareness

I want to finish this chapter by bringing you back to thinking about the levels of awareness mentioned in the Introduction. The context in that section was the client's learning, but they also apply to your own learning. Distractions are predominantly in your level one awareness: they are pretty easy to notice. But many of the other factors mentioned will be harder to locate. They will be spread between all of the levels.

Once you have identified some of these factors be prepared for it to take time and practice before you are able to change the way they influence or impact on your coaching. Some will be easy to change, others less so. You might find that you work down through the levels over time. As you notice and get to grips with handling the easier factors you start to notice and learn to handle the more deep-rooted ones. Over time the ones that continue to influence your coaching are likely to stem from your level four awareness and perhaps surface less often in your practice. These are likely to be much harder to surface without some kind of external intervention.

Reflective questions

- What do you know about yourself already that has the potential to influence or impact on your coaching?

- Knowing what you know about your own personality preferences, how might these show up in your coaching?

- What aspects of your upbringing inform the person that you are today? How might this be influencing your coaching?

- How does your internal dialogue impact on your coaching?

- Take one of the above answers and look out for it in your coaching. Use this as a focus for your reflective practice. What happened? What was the impact of this? Then decide what you will do differently, if anything, as a result of your reflection.

- Think about one section of a recent coaching session. Break down what happened, or what you believe may have happened, into stages in the same way that I have broken down the personal experiences on pages 49 and 53. What does this tell you about the values, beliefs, assumptions or judgements that may have been informing your coaching?

- How often are your own solutions informing your coaching intervention?

- What are you doing to develop your awareness of the factors that are impacting on your coaching?

Invisible Coach mode

03

You are not the invisible coach. The invisible coach is found within the client: the invisible coach is the client's own inner wisdom. You are just the person who is helping your clients find and strengthen their inner invisible coach.

Every one of us has this well of inner wisdom. The modes of presence are you tapping into your well so that you can help clients to tap into theirs. The invisible coach is within each and every one of us.

The key words for Invisible Coach mode are:

- listen;
- silence;
- patience;
- trust;
- brevity; and
- simplicity.

Invisible Coach mode is the first of four modes of coaching presence. This is the mode where the client's own invisible coach is able to surface and flourish. In this mode you are encouraging clients to focus on themselves and to access their own innate wisdom. You are encouraging them to explore the topic in free flow and independently. You are providing a space where the clients can take the time to uncover what they know about the topic, a space where they can slow down and deepen their thinking.

You wait patiently while they access their levels of awareness. To start off with they may access their level one awareness, which may include information that in the normal day-to-day run of things remains just out of reach. With more time and space they start to access information from the lower levels of awareness.

Invisible Coach mode is the first mode and is also the base mode. It will often be the starting point of any coaching and it is the mode that you keep returning to throughout the coaching. When you have used an intervention from one of the other modes of presence you come back to Invisible Coach mode to give clients time and space to assimilate, consider, think through and decide what they think either about, or as a result of, the intervention.

Figure I.2 in the Introduction offers a way to think about how you are being in each of the four modes of presence. In Invisible Coach mode you have an almost ghostly presence. You are there but barely visible. You are not adding anything of yourself to interventions. You are not interpreting or making meaning of anything the client says. For most of the time that you are in Invisible Coach mode you want the client to almost forget that you are there. However, being completely invisible defeats the object. Your presence is quiet and unobtrusive but it is also very tangible. Your presence and focused attention are what makes the difference between the client being able to think through their topic fully or not.

In Invisible Coach mode you use the bare minimum and simplest of interventions. Coach input is kept to a minimum and there is maximum

Remember the driving metaphor from the Introduction. The coach is the passenger, the client the driver. Both know the destination, or at least the approximate destination, but the driver makes all the choices about how to get there. Which way to turn at the crossroads, which roads to take, including detours; the driver might decide to stop off at places of interest along the way. The passenger enjoys the ride, and observes some of the things that he or she notice along the way. The passenger is interested in the choices the driver makes about the route, how he or she makes the choices and what the driver takes account of and what he or she ignores, but doesn't mention these for the time being. The passenger trusts the driver and enjoys the ride, but he or she is paying attention in case the driver gets lost along the way.

client input. Less is more when using this mode. You don't need to know about processes, tools, models or theories, or to have any views, opinions or knowledge. When you do speak, you keep it short and you replay words or actions that the client has used. You are replaying things back to the client that you notice along the way. You are acting as a mirror reflecting back to the client.

Silence is one of the most common interventions used, but it is not a passive activity. Without your presence, it is unlikely that the client will be able to explore as deeply or as widely. You may not be saying much but you are paying attention, listening, observing, noticing, noting and being curious. Kline (1999; 2009) refers to it as 'providing a thinking environment'.

Why choose Invisible Coach mode

The key reasons for choosing Invisible Coach mode are to:

1 establish the foundations for the clients' learning;

2 raise clients' awareness of their inner wisdom;

3 build client confidence in their own invisible coach;

4 help clients access their invisible coach outside of the coaching;

5 avoid some emotional barriers;

6 limit the impact or influence of the coach's factors in the coaching; and

7 gather information to use later.

1. Establish the foundations for the client's learning

When using Invisible Coach mode, particularly at the start of coaching, both clients and coach start to learn something about where the clients are in their learning at the minute. You are establishing the current state of play in the clients' level of knowledge and awareness of the topic. If the intent in coaching is to achieve transformational change we need to help clients to identify and build on their current strengths, knowledge and awareness. There's no significant transformation if all the clients do is work out what they know already. In this mode you are establishing what the client is capable of right now. You are learning about the client and starting to notice and identify where the gaps in knowledge and awareness might rest and where the opportunity for transformation might lie.

2. Raise clients' awareness of their own inner wisdom

You know that the clients have resources available within themselves – everyone has a deep well of inner wisdom. Clients often know so much more and are much more capable than they give themselves credit for. However, when they arrive at the coaching they are not always aware of this and as a result they do not access their knowledge or resources. To build and expand their learning we want clients to realize just how knowledgeable they already are. In Invisible Coach mode you invite the clients to learn this about themselves. You want to help them to bring as much of the information that lies in their deeper levels of awareness into focus for themselves. You know that they have an inner wisdom and their own invisible coach, and you want them to become aware of it too.

3. Build client confidence in their own invisible coach

Sometimes people arrive at coaching having lost some of the confidence in their own inner wisdom. They are too busy and don't always have time to think about things adequately. As a result they get unexpected or unwelcome outcomes and this can knock their confidence. Their faith in their thinking or their judgement is lost.

Regardless of preferred learning styles people are much more confident in implementing their learning when they have drawn conclusions for themselves. People are well equipped to make their own judgements. When they do so they are more confident about their chosen course of action and there is a greater likelihood of change taking place outside of the coaching as a result.

So we use Invisible Coach mode to help clients to remember that they can think well and draw their own conclusions and rebuild their confidence in their own thinking. Some people may need to be provided with more information than others but you help them to use their own judgement to decide the merits of what they need to do.

4. Help clients access their own invisible coach outside of the coaching

Coaching stimulates different types of learning. First there is the topic-related learning that comes through the exploration and the new conclusions that are drawn by clients. This includes the learning clients make about themselves and their wider system.

Then there is the second-order learning that can be achieved by the clients. They learn *how* they learn in the coaching sessions. I have often been told by clients that they have used some of the tools and techniques that I use with them with their own teams. They will learn, by your demonstration of it, how to use Invisible Coach mode with their own people to help them to think more deeply.

Second-order learning also includes the clients learning how to tap into their own inner wisdom without the need for a coach. They realize that in their coaching sessions they can usually access more information than they first think, so they get into the habit of looking for this additional information independently. When they are confident in their thinking ability, they will think more widely and broadly when they are not with us. If they learn how to access their own invisible coach when they are with us then they have a better chance of doing so in situations when they are not. We use Invisible Coach mode to help clients to learn to use their own invisible coach.

5. Avoid some emotional barriers

Sometimes when working with clients you will come across barriers and resistance. Often emotional barriers need to be managed before any exploration can continue. People can be very resistant to being told what to do – very good ideas or suggestions can be thrown out purely because they did not come up with the idea themselves. Even when clients ask for advice they will very often find reasons why it doesn't apply to them. Eventually they may take things on board but the resistance needs to be overcome first.

You can avoid or get around this resistance by using Invisible Coach mode. If you are allowing the clients to explore whatever they need to, and to choose the direction of travel, and to come up with their own ideas and suggestions and draw their own conclusions, then you are not going to come across these barriers or resistance. Clients may identify something as a barrier for themselves and choose to explore it, in which case there's no resistance. They open the door for themselves to deal with. If the clients are choosing the direction of travel they will go where they feel they are willing and able to go, and you have fewer emotional barriers to deal with later.

6. Limit the impact or influence of coach's factors in the coaching

The factors that might impact or influence our coaching were discussed in Chapter 2. A bonus in using Invisible Coach mode is that you don't have to worry about so many of the factors influencing or impacting on the coaching. In this mode you do not think about your own views or opinions while coaching. You're not concerned with process, tools, models, theories or technique to use and you're not thinking about what to do next. You are focusing all of your attention on tuning in to the client, listening, observing, noticing, noting, etc and because of this there is less likelihood that other factors will impact or influence you.

7. Gather information to use later

The final reason for using Invisible Coach mode is to gather information for later. You will be noticing metaphors, gaps in their exploration, aspects that they might be ignoring or avoiding, questions that have been raised in your mind, limiting beliefs, etc. You will be filing this information in order to be able to retrieve it later.

Beliefs

If you are going to be effective in Invisible Coach mode there are certain beliefs in addition to those mentioned in the Introduction that will make a difference. You need to believe that:

- Your clients have an innate wisdom that they have not yet accessed (they have their own invisible coach within them).

- The clients know much more about the situation than has been shared so far.

- Whatever and however they choose to explore the topic is right for the clients.

- You do not always have to lead the exploration in a coaching relationship.

- You can work with clients without having to influence them in any way.

- Sometimes it's okay to not understand or even know what the client is talking about. It's okay to coach while not knowing.

- Silence is an intervention in itself. Just being an attentive listener can make a profound difference to the clients' exploration.

- The less they focus on you as a coach the more attention they can pay to the topic under exploration.

How to achieve Invisible Coach mode

In this section I offer you some hints and tips for achieving Invisible Coach mode. Remember when reading this section that it relates only to this mode. There will be times when these courses of action are not appropriate, in which case you move into another mode of presence:

1 Decide to use Invisible Coach mode.
2 Trust the clients.
3 Let go of thinking about tools and techniques.
4 Use silence.
5 Be curious.
6 Listen with your whole body.
7 Be comfortable with not knowing.
8 Do not interrupt.
9 Be unobtrusive.
10 Follow the clients' line of enquiry.
11 Replay the clients' own language back to them.
12 Replay non-verbal information back to clients.
13 Wait for the eyes.
14 Enjoy the clients' resourcefulness.

1. Decide to use Invisible Coach mode

As mentioned in the Introduction, the first thing that you will have done is assessed which of the four modes of presence will be most helpful to the client in the moment. You make the decision to use Invisible Coach mode. It should also be an automatic decision to go into Invisible Coach mode after every intervention, to give the clients time and space to consider this in the context of their exploration.

2. Trust the clients

You trust the clients to explore what needs to be explored. You trust that they have a wide range of information available to them that you are yet to see and you let them seek it for themselves. If the clients digress or go off on a tangent and you don't know whether this relates to the topic, you trust that it is useful to the clients and go with it.

3. Let go of thinking about tools and techniques

In Invisible Coach mode you use very few interventions and then only the simplest. For the moment you have no need for most of the tools and techniques that you have learnt. Free yourself from using them. Let go of thinking about what interventions you are going to use and just let your curiosity inform anything you say. If you need to encourage clients to continue with their exploration your curiosity will provide you with your intervention. Let go of your own thoughts and opinions rather than allowing them to influence your interventions.

4. Use silence

In Invisible Coach mode you are providing clients with the time and space to access their own inner wisdom and trusting them to be able to think it through and draw their own conclusions. Silence is the key intervention that enables this to happen. Your silence allows the clients time to explore the topic. In the silence you are focusing all of your attention on the clients. You are genuinely interested in what they have to say, while keeping yourself out of their way. This focused attention is key to facilitating their exploration. Without an attentive listener people can't think in the same way.

Be patient and wait for the clients to indicate that they are ready for you to say something again. Be comfortable with their silence. You can tell by watching someone when they are still thinking, so be quiet, wait patiently and allow them to decide when they are ready for you to intervene. Even then, don't say anything immediately. If you wait just a little longer before you speak you may well find that they pick up the exploration and develop it further without you having to say anything at all. Patiently wait until the client is ready to invite you back in to speak.

5. Be curious

Curiosity and silence are two of your best friends. I've mentioned silence so what do I mean by 'be curious'? Before you can start being curious you need to focus all of your attention on the clients, what they are saying, doing and all the little nuances. Be interested enough to look for all the tiny clues that they might be providing about what's informing their thinking. The curious bit is then being really interested in what's informing or influencing their thinking or what's happening in their physicality. What do all those little clues mean? You do this without trying to interpret or make any meaning of these for yourself. You just… wonder…. To help clients deepen and broaden their exploration you express your curiosity; for example, 'What made you smile just then?'

6. Listen with your whole body

Active listening is enhanced if you listen with your whole body and not just with your ears and head. Clients will be using their physicality while they are talking and this will be outside of their awareness. This physicality will give you clues as to what they are talking about, insights that you can use either now or later. While listening move your body in the same way as the client (without being too obvious!) Use your arms, legs, head or body to reflect the clients' movement. Feel what they are feeling through the movement. You can also gain insights through imagining yourself moving your body in the same way. Through this movement, or imagined movement, you can notice which words carry more emphasis than others, or you can identify the possible emotions or feeling that are associated with the words that they are using.

In one of our sessions a client's exploration had slowed down. While she had been talking I noticed that she had repeatedly used the word 'preparation'. I replayed the word back to her, and there was no particular response. She used the word again and this time I imagined myself mirroring her body language and I felt weighed down. She seemed ready for another input from me so I mentioned her repetition of the word and how heavy it felt when she said it. This time it triggered a response. From this she went on to think about how heavily she had prepared for a particular piece of work and the lack of appreciation that she had received in return. She went on to explore the fact that this imbalance between effort and reward was a common theme for her. Replaying the word 'preparation' back to her earlier had not triggered a response. The reference to the weight behind it was the trigger. If I had not imagined myself using her body language I would have missed this vital piece of information. This use of Invisible Coach mode was enough to take her thinking in a new direction and for her to explore something she had not considered before.

7. Be comfortable with not knowing

When in Invisible Coach mode you will not always know what is being talked about or why it's being talked about, but the client will know. You might be confused but the client seems clear so you do not seek clarification. If you think clients have gone off on a tangent, or are talking about something completely unrelated and you don't know why, let them get on with it. You may make a note of these things to pick up later using a different mode, but for the time being you leave it be. You remain comfortable with not knowing.

A simple example is when clients are using jargon that you don't understand. It may be specific to the company they work for. The client knows what they are talking about. You want to ask them what they mean. Your intervention is more to do with satisfying your need to know rather than widening or deepening their exploration so is best left alone for the time being.

8. Do not interrupt

This one is simple. As long as clients are talking or thinking you do not interrupt them. Interruption is something that you may use in Visible Coach mode, but not now. Another way of thinking about this is to wait until clients 'invite' you to speak again – not literally, but you can see the invitation in their eyes and body language.

9. Be unobtrusive

In Chapter 1 I talked about sitting near enough to clients to be able observe them closely, but out of their line of sight. This is to support you in being unobtrusive in Invisible Coach mode. You stay out of their line of sight so that you don't draw their attention away from the exploration. When you offer an intervention keep it short and to the point, to minimize the amount of time they spend away from the exploration.

It also involves not making any movements or sounds that might distract clients while they are thinking. You keep your body movements and sounds to a minimum. Making any kind of noise while they are doing their deep thinking can distract them, as shown in this example.

I was using Invisible Coach mode while a client of mine explored her topic. She had been doing so for at least five minutes and was engrossed in the exploration. She said something, contradicted herself and then laughed at the contradiction.

I could see the irony in what she'd just said and I laughed too. It was only a quiet laugh but it was loud enough for her to hear me. It stopped her in her tracks. She immediately stopped her exploration and asked why I had laughed. When I told her that I had laughed with her, she was surprised as she had not realized that she had laughed. She now wanted to know what I thought of what she'd said, and whether I agreed with her. Her train of thought was not only interrupted but shifted by my accidental intervention. Inadvertently I had moved into Visible Coach mode by interrupting her train of thought, and in this case it did not aid the client's thinking. The exploration was not complete so I encouraged her to continue but it took a little while for her to settle back down into this.

10. Follow the clients' line of enquiry

You do not choose the direction of travel nor do you try to change it without the idea having first originated with the client. You follow the clients' line of enquiry. When you offer interventions you encourage them to continue along their own train of thought. The intervention may involve a change of direction, but only if they have already mentioned it in their exploration. For example, you may notice clients ask a question but you know that they are not asking you. Sometimes they will preface it with something like, 'The question is…' or they add a questioning tone to a statement. You notice the question. Sometimes they start to explore the answer to the question, other times they don't. If they choose to continue with the exploration without addressing the question they just asked, then wait while they finish this particular line of enquiry. When they come to a stop and 'invite' you to speak again, you could choose to remind them of the question that they asked themselves earlier. It is a change of direction but the idea originated in their thinking, not yours.

A simple way of following clients' line of enquiry is to ask them what the next question should be. As the coach you don't have to work out all the questions. You can use Invisible Coach mode and get clients to decide where to take the coaching now by asking them, 'What would be the most useful question for me to ask next?'

11. Replay the clients' own language back to them

When clients pause in their thinking you can help to move their exploration simply by replaying their own words back to them. Hearing their own words can help then to confirm, clarify, question, affirm, organize, delve, open up and reconsider their thinking and so much more. Think of yourself as an action replay button on the TV: you show clients what happened, they do the analysis. This is where your curiosity informs your interventions. You replay words that you are curious about back to clients.

When replaying words you use the exact words the clients used, either singly or in groups of words and without adding any commentary of your own. You might also replay how you observed them using language; for example repetition of words, heavier weighting on words, or contradictory words. If you do this, state only what you notice, for example, 'I notice you have used the word (insert exact word) quite often.' You might be curious about what you perceive to be a contradiction but keep your assessment that it is a contradiction out of it (at least in this mode). Let them work out what it means to them – it may not be contradictory at all!

Another point here on the subject of jargon: always use the clients' jargon and not your own. You might know it by another name, but to maintain Invisible Coach mode you need to stick with theirs. If you use your own jargon, you may end up having to explain yourself and you've inadvertently moved into another mode.

12. Replay non-verbal information back to clients

Look out for physical changes in their body. What changes are you curious about? The mind and body do not work in isolation and the body provides clues about what might be happening in the mind. Many clues are only there for a fraction of a second before they disappear, so you need to be paying close attention to spot them. When you do, point these out without commentary or judgement. For example: 'I noticed a small twitch at the side of your mouth when you said that', 'I noticed when you mentioned (person's name) that their name seemed to get caught in your throat', 'I notice that you've started tapping your foot and you've gone quite red in the face.' These are all actual examples that when pointed out have resulted in one of my clients taking her exploration in a different direction. The twitch in the mouth turned out to be a question about whether she had got enough facts about the situation. The catch in the throat turned out to be a question over whether the person really was the right person to approach. The red face and tapping foot are detailed below.

A client I was working with was exploring her longer-term career plans. She was calm and relaxed. Nothing untoward had been mentioned, all of what she was talking about seemed very reasonable. There was no suggestion of a problem.

All of a sudden her face turned red and her foot started bouncing up and down: she seemed really agitated. It was in stark contrast to her demeanour so far. So I pointed out the changes that I had noticed adding no commentary. I just said, 'I notice you have gone very red, and your foot is bouncing. What happened there?' It had suddenly occurred to her that she wants to start a family within the next two to three years and that this was an important factor that she had overlooked in her exploration. This thought was accompanied by a very clear change in her physicality. The next intervention was based on following her line of enquiry: 'So how does this impact on your thinking?'

13. Wait for the eyes

Pay attention to the clients' eyes: they can provide you with all sorts of information. Examples include being able to tell when they are still thinking (even if they are not saying anything), when they are having an internal conversation with themselves or when they are feeling an emotion. You might include what's happening in the eyes in the information you replay back to the client: 'I noticed your eyes darting about just then, what was happening for you?' 'I notice your eyes welling up as you were talking about that.'

Their eyes will also let you know when they are ready for you to speak again. When they are exploring most clients (but not all of them) will look everywhere except at you. When they get to a pause in their thinking, they look to you. In Invisible Coach mode you wait for this to happen before you offer an intervention.

14. Enjoy the clients' resourcefulness

Finally, enjoy being with and observing clients. Quietly (or openly) appreciate their resourcefulness, their thinking capacity, their turn of phrase, how they articulate themselves, their knowledge, their expertise, their humour, their abilities, their honesty and whatever else you can find to appreciate and enjoy about them.

Things you may notice

A key indicator for choosing Invisible Coach mode in the moment is how much information you have heard first-hand from your client, whether at the beginning of a session or the beginning of a new intervention. The less you have heard the greater the chance that Invisible Coach mode is most appropriate.

When you are successfully using Invisible Coach mode you will notice that you are saying and doing very little: clients will be doing the vast majority of the talking. Mostly you will be sitting quietly and saying nothing. You might notice that you forget to think about tools, techniques or models: you are just enjoying the clients' exploration.

You may notice that clients look as if they are in their own world. They are so engrossed in their exploration that they don't appear to notice anything else in the room, you included. They are talking and thinking and you can hear them considering different aspects of the topic on their own. You can hear them moving their exploration on themselves. You are hearing lots of different information coming from different perspectives. They barely need any encouragement from you to continue their exploration, just a few words or the odd question is enough to get them going again.

You may notice quite a few silences during the session, when neither of you is talking. When silent you can see that clients are still thinking. They might look as if they are searching for something, sometimes you will see their eyes darting about, but you can tell that the focus is still in their head and not elsewhere. Sometimes they just carry on thinking without talking. They look as if they might have forgotten you are there listening to them.

They might be looking everywhere except at you. Their eyes might move around the room and rest on something specifically but you can sense that they are not seeing it. If you do choose a different mode and interrupt their flow you might notice a look of surprise on their face, when they remember that you are still here!

Inadvertent use of Invisible Coach mode

As mentioned in the Introduction, inadvertent use of the modes of presence happens when we don't realize that we are doing it. We use it by accident rather than by design. Using it by accident doesn't necessarily equate to using it in error. The aim of this book is to help you to be more conscious in your choices and in doing so increase the odds of using the most appropriate intervention in the moment rather than relying on chance.

With Invisible Coach mode there are fewer ways of it being used inadvertently than in some of the other modes of presence. It takes a measure of composure and calmness to be able to minimize your interventions in coaching, which can make it harder to do by accident. But I do have a couple of things for you to consider in your reflective practice.

Before I mention these I am conscious that it may be that you have developed a quiet, patient and often silent way of working with your client without any prior knowledge of the Invisible Coach mode. As a result you may naturally move into this presence without thinking about it – it has already moved into your unconscious competence repertoire. This does not make it inadvertent. If you are reflecting on this aspect the question to ask is, 'Is this a conscious choice I am making?'

- When you chose Invisible Coach mode, could you have articulated what you were doing or why you were doing it? If you couldn't have answered either of these questions in the moment then it may be inadvertent use of the mode.

- What other options did you consider in the moment? Did you rule out the other three modes of presence before you chose this one? This applies to all of the modes of presence. If you haven't considered using the other three modes of presence first, your use of this mode may be inadvertent.

- Do you always wait for the client to give you an opening to speak? This is a definite indicator of inadvertent use of Invisible Coach mode. When growing up most of us learnt that it is rude to interrupt when someone is talking so most of us wait patiently for our turn to speak. When coaching there are times when it is appropriate to interrupt the client (see Chapter 6 on the Visible Coach mode). If you never interrupt and always wait your turn to speak then consider through your reflective practice that you might be inadvertently using Invisible Coach mode.

- Occasionally we don't know what to say next, so we say nothing. As coaches we're often pretty good at handling silence, but many of our clients are not and will feel a compulsion to fill the gap. Often this will mean that they continue their exploration, even if we have given them the space by default. We might feel a bit awkward but clients may not have noticed, or better still think you did it deliberately. When this happens you probably get away with it. But if it doesn't, the inadvertent use of the mode could interrupt the flow of the coaching temporarily.

- Choosing *not* to challenge clients may also be inadvertent use of Invisible Coach mode. You allow them to continue their own exploration but this may be related to your discomfort about a potentially difficult aspect of the clients' exploration. Be careful that you are not using Invisible Coach mode as an excuse for not going there. I touch on this further under 'Risks', below.

- Finally, if you get distracted (as discussed in Chapter 2) clients may continue with their exploration because you are silent, but you miss what they are saying. In this case you are not in Invisible Coach mode, you are absent!

Risks

You could coach a client using only Invisible Coach mode. Occasionally it will be appropriate to do so, but it is unlikely to be appropriate to do so regularly with the same client. Coaching from any one of the modes of presence comes with some risks. Here are the reasons why you may not want to conduct an entire coaching session using Invisible Coach mode:

1 The client can miss out on valuable insights.
2 Limit the potential effectiveness of solutions.
3 Perpetuate old beliefs or patterns of behaviour.
4 Negative cycle.
5 Unethical behaviour is affirmed.
6 Loss of attention to the process.

1. Miss out on valuable insights

In Invisible Coach mode clients choose what they explore in the coaching session. This also means that they choose what *not* to explore. There may be aspects that they are missing or choosing to avoid. There are often good reasons in the clients' mind why they don't want to go there. It may mean having to face up to something that is quite difficult for them, having to deal with emotions they would rather avoid, having to change their thinking about something, or admitting to something they would rather not admit – or a multitude of other reasons.

Often there is the potential for profound and transformational learning in these difficult aspects. The best learning can be gained when clients are outside their comfort zone. When determining their own exploration clients will often stay within their comfort zone. If the coach lets them continue to avoid aspects that are uncomfortable for whatever reason, clients may miss out on some valuable insights and learning. This could then limit their potential for growth and development. Choosing not to challenge is to do clients a disservice. In addition, you have a wealth of expertise, experience and knowledge. If you do not add anything of yourself to the coaching relationship, clients can miss any learning they might gain from your experience.

2. Limit the potential effectiveness of solutions

Any solutions that clients settle upon through the sole use of Invisible Coach mode may be flawed. Every perspective or lens through which clients explore the topic will open up or close down potential solutions. The more perspectives from which they have explored the topic, the greater the likelihood that any solutions arrived at will fix the issue without causing new or different problems. If clients have chosen their direction of travel and in doing so have missed out on exploring the topic from one or more perspectives, they run the risk of not noticing other possible options, or not shutting down defective options.

I find that the more potential options clients can identify, the greater the chance of them finding a great solution that doesn't cause new problems. Under their own steam clients can sometimes think in extremes – it is an either/or situation. In my experience the real answer lies somewhere in between. There are nearly always other options that have not been considered, and it is usually one of the later ideas on a brainstorming list that is the best solution. When it comes to generating ideas clients will often stop after one or two ideas, or when they have an idea that they think sounds feasible. It's unusual for clients to come up with a wide range of options without several interventions from the coach. If we stay in Invisible Coach mode we potentially limit the range of ideas clients can come up with.

Any potential solutions that emerge usually require some scrutiny or analysis before determining whether they are the best; exploration from a range of perspectives is usually needed. When choosing their own direction of travel clients will often fail to pay attention to this scrutiny, or aspects of it. If we don't facilitate that exploration they may miss something in the analysis. All of this – the missing out of perspectives, the curtailed brainstorming of ideas or the lack of analysis of the solution – may result in clients arriving at a solution that is inappropriate, mediocre, or one that solves one problem but causes another.

3. Perpetuate old beliefs or patterns of behaviour

There will be aspects that clients cannot see. They will not notice things like outdated values, beliefs, assumptions or judgements as these are often deep in their level four awareness. They probably don't know that they exist. They won't follow this direction of travel in their exploration because they don't know it's an option. It won't matter how long we stay in Invisible Coach mode, clients will not see what they can't see. If we don't help them to see these outdated values and beliefs they remain intact, and potentially continue to impede the client's progress.

4. Negative cycle

If you are working with people who are feeling particularly negative at the moment, remaining in Invisible Coach mode is unlikely to help. If they've had a really bad day, and it feels like nothing is going right, they find it hard to see the positive aspects of anything. Their mind is closed to particular viewpoints. Their thinking becomes constricted and their mind is not open to possibility or creativity. They only see the downsides of everything. People who are in this state of mind find it hard to get out of this way of thinking on their own. When you notice that your client is on this cycle of negativity you need to move out of Invisible Coach mode to facilitate a change in their thinking.

5. Unethical behaviour is affirmed

Everyone has a different set of values and what is ok with some people is not ok with others. Sometimes clients may talk about doing something that you and others (including their employer or the law) might conceive as being unethical or illegal. If you remain in Invisible Coach mode and do not challenge their exploration of unethical aspects, clients may perceive this as an affirmation. They may read into your lack of challenge your agreement with their course of action, and then go ahead with the unethical behaviour.

This also has the potential to result in a challenge to your reputation as a coach. Clients may use this as part of their defence – they told the coach about it and the coach said it was ok. (You might not have said it was ok, but you didn't say that it wasn't!) Even if it is not mentioned in the written contract there may be an expectation from the organization paying for your work that you will dissuade clients from carrying out any unethical behaviour that might be discussed with you (see psychological contract, CIPD, 2013). You'll have a hard job defending yourself if you did not challenge the thinking during the coaching.

6. Loss of attention to process

When you are focusing so much of your attention on the client, enjoying his or her resourcefulness and being curious about everything, it's really easy to forget to pay attention to other things, such as managing the coaching process and timekeeping. In Invisible Coach mode you let go of so much of your usual thinking that this can include process aspects if you are not careful. In enjoying the moment it's easy for time to just slip by.

Reflective questions

- Think about a recent coaching session. There were probably times when you would now describe your presence as Invisible Coach mode. Identify one point when this happened. What happened in the lead up to this intervention? Why did you choose this mode in that moment? What impact did it have on your client? In hindsight what makes this the right intervention? And what makes it the wrong intervention?

- Based on this experience how will you know next time that Invisible Coach mode might be appropriate? What might you do differently to enhance your use of Invisible Coach mode next time?

- When you put into practice the new behaviour that you identified in the previous question what happened? What was the impact for the client? Perhaps let the client know what you did differently and ask him or her how it impacted on them? What do you conclude from this?

- What needs to happen next for you to enhance your use of Invisible Coach mode in your coaching?

- Consider how often you interrupt or challenge your clients. When was the last time you did this?

- In your reflective practice pay attention to whether or how often you interrupt or challenge your clients about difficult issues and emotions. Is there a chance you are inadvertently using Invisible Coach mode by not doing either of these? What needs to change in your coaching practice?

Emergent Coach mode

04

The key words for Emergent Coach mode are:

- stimulate;
- elevate;
- expand;
- magnify;
- detachment;
- creativity; and
- perseverance.

Refer back to Figure I.2 in the Introduction to see how you are changing your presence slightly for this mode. The difference is in your style of interventions. In Invisible Coach mode clients choose what they explore and how they explore the topic with no guidance from you. In Emergent Coach mode you are providing a means for clients to continue their exploration of the topic, a means that enables and strengthens their own invisible coach. You invite them to use various tools and techniques that will help them to explore the topic from different channels of perception, to stimulate them to think differently about the topic. It is in this mode that you can use your most creative interventions, tools or techniques (see Chapter 7 for some ideas). You still do not add anything of yourself in the interventions.

Your intention when using Emergent Coach is to help clients access new information. The purpose is to help them to enrich the information they have already gained through your use of other modes of presence. Your aim is to help them to explore in more detail, and to see beyond the edges of their current vision. You are expanding their level two awareness and taking them into level three awareness.

In Emergent Coach mode your intention is also to help clients to take some of the subjectivity or emotional attachment out of their exploration. If they are immersed in the topic, or feeling emotional about it, it can cloud their thinking. Your intention is to elevate them out of the situation or the emotion (without removing it) so that they can take a more detached and objective view of either the topic or the learning that is within the emotion.

Your interventions are designed to invite clients to explore the topic from a variety of channels of perception that they have not yet considered. This might include stakeholders (see the Glossary) or interested parties. You are inviting clients to listen to all the parties in the situation; you help clients identify who the interested parties are and then invite them into the room (virtually speaking) so the client can 'hear' their views and opinions. Part of making sure that the views and needs of all interested parties are attended to may include making sure that clients attend to their own needs and aspirations. Some people spend their time thinking of others without consideration for their own needs.

In the same way as in Invisible Coach mode, you are maintaining a stance where you leave your own views and opinions about the topic out of the conversation. In Invisible Coach mode you use the clients' language by replaying this back to them in your interventions. In Emergent Coach mode you use what you are hearing, seeing and feeling to inform your interventions. The clients' language, or the perspectives they are choosing or missing, or what you notice about their emotions (discussed in more detail later) might inform your choice of intervention.

While interventions in Invisible Coach mode are very simple and brief in nature, interventions used in Emergent Coach mode will sometimes need to

---

Continuing the car metaphor from the Introduction you are still the passenger but now you are offering the driver a new map to have a look at. Perhaps the existing map is an A–Z of the local area and the new one is an ordnance survey map covering a bigger region. The A–Z contains limited information about a particular location: the roads, rivers, railway lines, towns, etc. The ordnance survey map contains all of these plus footpaths, fields, buildings, hills including the gradients, mineshafts, wells, etc. It is larger in scale, covers a wider area and contains much more detail. You are encouraging the driver to look at what is essentially the same map but contains much more information that will inform his or her decisions.

be explained to clients before they can use them to continue their exploration. They will often be quite novel so some clients may be resistant to the idea because they are not used to thinking in this way. Many of the interventions will take some time before they are utilized fully to aid the clients' exploration. You may need to remind them of the intervention several times before they are explored fully. You may need to persevere to encourage clients to stick with it.

Why choose Emergent Coach mode

1 Because you know the client knows more.

2 To enrich the clients' exploration of the topic.

3 To bring greater objectivity to the exploration.

4 To open up potential new and different solutions.

5 To increase the clients' return on investment.

1. Because you know the client knows more

My experience is that people know far more than they realize. Their mind and body stores a vast wealth of information and a huge proportion of this information has been assimilated by the brain outside of their day-to-day awareness so they don't realize it is there. It's like an iceberg: most of the iceberg is below the surface of the water, and even though neither you nor the client can see it at the moment, you know it is there. We disrespect our clients if we assume that the smidgen of information that they have accessed solely through Invisible Coach mode is the full extent of their information or resources. If we know that one of the ways in which clients build their confidence is through realizing just how much they know already, then we need to be patient and continue to help clients establish this, help them explore the iceberg below the surface. We use Emergent Coach mode to increase substantially the amount of information that is brought into the clients' awareness. It can bring about a much deeper level of understanding.

2. Enrich the clients' exploration of the topic

From the exploration so far clients may already have a greater awareness about the topic than when they first arrived at the coaching but it would be unusual if this was the full picture. There is likely to be relevant information missing. They will have missed particular perspectives and angles that contain other information that impacts or influences the system and is useful to them when drawing their conclusions. As the coach you have a better vantage point than clients to observe the perspectives they are using. You notice the gaps in their exploration and where they might be narrowing their view. From the outside you can see the wider system that they are not yet paying any attention to. You can see other vantage points that clients may or may not be aware of. Before they draw their conclusions you help them enrich their exploration, by exchanging the map for a better and bigger one so that they can fill in more of the detail and explore what's beyond their current map in the periphery of their vision.

3. Bring greater objectivity to the exploration

Sometimes clients are too close to the topic to be able to see it clearly. They can't see the wood for the trees. Their proximity distorts their way of thinking about it and it can become very subjective. Other times there can be a high emotional attachment to the topic which also clouds the view. In Emergent Coach mode you help clients step further away from the topic and explore it in a more detached way. They can see the topic more clearly and as a result draw more objective conclusions.

4. Open up potential new and different solutions

When people come up with solutions based on a limited view of the topic, they often find that the solution fails or causes unforeseen problems. The solution is flawed because the perspectives they have not looked at have an impact on the solution. When clients have formed a rich understanding of the topic through a detailed and thorough exploration, which includes the wider context, they have a much firmer foundation on which to base their decisions about potential solutions or changes in behaviour. All of the new information will have a bearing on the topic. It can either reinforce or dispel aspects of their current thinking, or move their thinking in some way or generate new thinking. It can have the same effect on determining any potential solutions or changes in behaviour. Sometimes just seeing the topic from another perspective opens up a new or different solution, or weakens or eliminates one that they have in mind. When they have taken a well-rounded view they are more likely to identify a wider range of potential solutions, and understand where and how some solutions might fall down. If the potential solutions are also analysed from a range of perspectives it will also provide a better chance of ensuring that the best solution is implemented.

5. Increase the clients' return on investment

Many of the interventions that you use in Emergent Coach mode can be used to some extent by clients on their own. When you facilitate clients' thinking through the use of tools and techniques, not only do they learn about the topic, they also learn about the various tools and techniques and how to use them. Some of the tools and techniques are easier to use alone than others, but they can still be used by clients to facilitate their own or other's thinking outside of the coaching relationship. They can use them to assess new situations and they are likely to make more informed decisions in the moment as a result. They also use the techniques when working with others and help others to make better decisions.

I actively encourage my clients to use these tools and techniques outside of the coaching. If the coaching is part of an ongoing programme, this expansion of their own thinking outside of the coaching programme will enable you to focus the coaching on greater, deeper and more transformational learning in the coaching sessions. The learning outcomes and therefore the return on their investment are enhanced.

Beliefs

The following are the beliefs that are specific to using Emergent Coach mode. These are in addition to the guiding beliefs in the Introduction:

- Clients know much more about the situation than they have shared so far, even if they do not realize it. If I help clients to draw out this information for themselves it will provide a stronger foundation on which to build a deeper overall learning experience. I am determined to make this the best learning experience it can be for clients.

- Some of the creative tools and techniques I could use will draw out far more information from the clients' own inner wisdom than could ever be achieved through 'talking or thinking interventions'.

- There are plenty of ways to draw information into clients' awareness that do not require me to be directive or share anything of myself. I would need much more information about the topic before any other type of intervention would effectively add to the clients' exploration.

- If I challenge or add information to the clients' exploration at this time it would be disrespectful of their intelligence and their capacity to think for themselves.

How to achieve Emergent Coach mode

Here are some things that you will typically use when you are aiming to achieve Emergent Coach mode:

1 Remind yourself of your reasons for choosing Emergent Coach mode.

2 Choose the type of channel of perception you want to offer the client.

3 Choose the intervention:
   - talk in the clients' language;
   - use interventions that place the topic in the space between you;
   - get creative;
   - introduce movement;
   - introduce stakeholders into the exploration;
   - introduce potential influences.

4 Finish the intervention.

1. Remind yourself of your reasons for using Emergent Coach mode

As with all of the modes of presence you will have made a deliberate decision to use Emergent Coach mode at the outset of the intervention. Many of the interventions used in this mode will take time for clients to explore fully – they can go off on tangents and it can be easy to get distracted from the intervention. It might be useful to remind yourself periodically of why you chose it and why you should remain in Emergent Coach mode until the client has exhausted this particular exploration.

2. Choose the type of channel of perception you want to offer the client

Emergent Coach mode is about encouraging different channels of perception and there is a wide variety to choose from (these are covered in more detail in Chapter 7). You are not going to have time in the coaching session to help the client to look at the topic from all of these available channels so before you decide your intervention ask yourself which type of channels of perception you think will help the client most in this moment. Remember that in Emergent Coach mode you are taking your steer from the client. It's about helping the client to explore more of what he or she knows already, so the channel chosen will be based on what you have heard (or not heard) the client talking about. What channels has the client mentioned but not yet explored? What channels has he or she not mentioned at all? What language has the client been using? Does this suggest any particular channels? Is the client emotive about the subject, or particularly logical? Would it help to take a more objective or subjective view of the topic? Once you know the type of channel you think will help the client it becomes easier to choose your intervention.

3. Choose the intervention

Once you know which channel of perception you are going to offer, this automatically reduces your choices of intervention, or tools and techniques. You can now consider the tools or techniques that fit with your choice of Emergent Coach mode and the channel that you want to help the client to explore. Quickly run through the list (to help you I have provided a range of possible options in Chapter 7). Which of the interventions do you feel/ sense is logical or right for the client? Here are some other aspects that will help you to decide.

Talk in the clients' language

When you are choosing interventions use the clients' language to inform your choices. While talking, clients will intersperse their exploration with similes and metaphors. They will talk about aspects of the topic as being like something (a simile) or as if they are something (a metaphor). For example, they might mention that they are 'like a small cog in a big wheel' (simile) or 'I'm bouncing around all over the place' (metaphor). These analogies can be really helpful when explored to help clients understand more about the topic and how they want things to be different. Notice these analogies and offer them back to clients in the form of a new channel of perception for the topic. On page 88 is an example of how I used a client's language to inform my choice of intervention.

Another way of talking in their language is to use some of the analytical tools and techniques that they are already familiar with. Clients may already be familiar with tools from theories on problem solving, leadership, creative thinking, service design, process mapping, quality control or

A client was feeling particularly low in a session. She is always hard on herself but today she was especially so. She'd said that she wanted to clarify her thinking and that she needed to pay more attention to what she was good at, but she didn't seem to be able to name anything positive about herself. Using Invisible Coach mode her mood was getting lower; I decided to try Emergent Coach mode. I had tentatively offered some people channels, but she was discounting these, so I also knew the same would happen if I shared my feelings on the subject. I had chosen a type of channel of perception. I knew that I wanted to help her to take a more objective viewpoint and to step out of the emotion that was clouding her view. I was looking for an appropriate intervention to help her to do this.

We carried on the exploration and she talked about the fact that when she wanted to help her daughter to feel more confident about the way she looks, she takes a photo of her and gets her to look at it and then she can see how good she looks. Here was the clue to my intervention. She needed the equivalent of a photograph to look at. I carry a selection of prints of paintings around with me so I brought these out and I invited her to pick one that represented her when she is doing a really good job. I invited her to look at this painting as if it was a photograph of her doing a good job. We then used it to pay attention to what she was good at. It surfaced a long list of great skills, and also highlighted for her the fact that the things she criticized herself for made up only a very small proportion of the whole. She was able to look at herself objectively and put aside the low mood that was clouding her judgement. She left the session feeling much more positive about herself.

marketing (some of these are mentioned in Chapter 7). Whatever their area of expertise there may be relevant tools and techniques that can be used as a lens to explore the current topic. Your clients may never have considered using them in the context of your discussion. For example a fishbone analysis (Ishikawa, 1990), which is commonly used in quality control or product design, can also be used to assess potential cause and effects in an interpersonal issue. The advantage of these is that you don't need to explain how to use the tool or technique because they know it already – all you have to do is encourage them to use it in this context.

Use interventions that place the topic in the space between you

In the example above one of the reasons why this worked is because the client was able to look at the picture to explore the topic. The topic was metaphorically moved from inside the client's head and placed in the space in front of her (on the table in this case). This enabled her to view the topic from an outside perspective. She was able to access more information than she could just by thinking about the topic.

Another aspect in the example is that she found it hard to express what she was good at because it would sound like she was boasting and this went against her beliefs. Using the picture enabled her to express things that she would otherwise not give a voice to. We first talked about the painting in terms of colours, lines, shapes, shades and contrast, and then explored what these represented in her.

There are plenty of tools and techniques that can be used to do this. They are ideal when you want to help clients take an outside in perspective, or to take the emotion out of the exploration, or when they are stuck. There is an old proverb (the origins of which I cannot determine): 'The fish is the last to notice the water'! You are trying to take clients out of the water (in a safe way!) so that they can notice it. You could ask them to take a helicopter view or a fly on the wall perspective. Or as in the example, use something like a picture and encourage the client to focus on this to represent the topic. Or get clients to write things down and then have a look at what they've written – anything that gets them to focus on something in front of them, rather than in their head. (Some ideas are included in Chapter 7.)

Get creative

Another way to help clients to access more information is by using tools and techniques to create something. Getting them to draw, paint, build or mould something, or even just play with toys or objects, encourages clients to engage different parts of their brain and as a result helps them to access new information and gain new insights.

Introduce movement

You can invite clients to access new information or to create a shift in their thinking through the use of movement. Invite them to embody the topic they are exploring in a shape or a way of moving. Invite them to move in a way that represents the topic as it is and/or how they would like it to be. If they do both then they can clearly see the difference between the two ways of moving. They know how to make the transition from one movement to the other and this will suggest changes that will help to make the transition in the topic.

When the client makes the change in the room, this will often translate into the change actually taking place. Here's an example of the first time I used movement with a client.

I was working with a young woman. She had an idea that she wanted to be self-employed but had no thoughts on what she would be doing in the business, which is how I came to be working with her. The first session was drawing to a close and seemed to have gone very well. We had started with the end in mind and explored what would it would be like when she had her own business already set up. This had generated some potential business ideas. I asked her about what she would do between this and the next session. She said she couldn't do anything at all. She couldn't even commit to thinking about what we'd talked about. We talked about it for a few minutes but she was adamant. I asked her what it felt like and she said it was like she couldn't move. I asked her where it was in her body that couldn't move and it was in her foot. Although I'd never done this before somehow I knew that if I could get her to move physically it would help to shift her thinking, so I invited her to stand up and demonstrate the resistance in her foot. She stood with one foot in front of the other as if she was taking a step but the back foot was rooted firmly to the floor. The dialogue went like this:

Maria: Show me how much you can move your back foot. (She lifted up her heel.) So where is your foot stuck?

Client: It's the ball of my foot that is stuck.

Maria: What other movement can you make with that foot?

Client: I can bring it to my other foot. (Which she did by dragging the ball of her foot along the floor.)

Maria: What other movement can you make?

Client: None.

Maria:　What's happening now?

Client:　I'm standing in front of a wall.

Maria:　And what can you see?

Client:　If I stand on my tiptoe I can see over the wall.

Maria:　Would you like to do that? (She stood on her tiptoes.) What can you do now?

Client:　I can look at all the things that are on the other side of the wall.

Maria:　What else can you do now?

Client:　I can see them and I can think about them.

Maria:　What else can you do?

Client:　Nothing, that's it.

Maria:　Does that feel enough?

Client:　Yes.

Once again I asked her what she would do between now and the next session and she said that she would have a look at and think about the options that we had discussed. That seemingly small shift that had been created in the coaching session was real and significant. I only worked with her for a short while, but the last time I heard about her she was setting up her business.

Introduce stakeholders into the exploration

While you are listening to clients, you notice any stakeholders or interested parties that they may mention. Look for those that are inside the organizational system (and don't forget the organization itself is a stakeholder): team members, other departments, other managers or directors. Notice people who are outside the organizational system but are linked to it: customers, investors, shareholders, suppliers, financiers. Also notice mentions of people in the client's personal system: they may be outside of the organization system but are touched by the fact that the client is part of it: family members including partners, children, parents, dependent relatives, and friends (see Chapter 7 for a fuller list). The client is unlikely to mention all of them, so notice who they don't mention. You are not likely to introduce all of them into the exploration, but there might be some key figures it would be useful to introduce. If you decide to use a people channel of perception you might ask the client to name the stakeholders or interested parties as a lead in to the intervention.

Introduce potential influences

Notice when clients mention (or don't mention) factors that might be influential to the topic or their exploration of it. These are likely to be external to the system and the influence may be subtle or overt. Examples include the sector in which the organization sits, eg construction, and the client's profession, eg accountancy (other examples are listed in Chapter 7). Don't forget the influence of the clients' own social groups, including church or community groups. What do they do outside of the organization that might influence their thinking? Invite clients to consider these influences in their exploration.

4. Finish the intervention

This might seem like an odd thing to say but I think it needs a mention. With some of these interventions, new information can be highlighted early on which can take the exploration off in a new direction and as a result leave some aspects unattended. To gain a fully rounded view of the topic, clients need to broadly finish the exploration using the intervention. For example, if you have encouraged them to draw the topic, they may have drawn elements of the topic, which has spurred their thinking, but there may be something important that hasn't been drawn yet. Encourage clients to finish off the intervention, in this example the drawing, before choosing which aspect of the exploration they want to move forward with. You might need to persevere with this. It might mean regularly reminding clients to come back to the original intervention when they digress.

Things you may notice

Before using Emergent Coach mode

Before you use Emergent Coach mode there are things you may notice in clients that might suggest this. Clients may seem to be running out of steam in their exploration. This can be seen by them repeating themselves or not being able to think of anything else they want to say about the topic.

Sometimes the exploration so far has been quite brief, but they don't think there's anything else to say about it.

They may also appear to be stuck in their thinking. They are struggling to find the words for what they want to say, they are indicating that that there is something to say but they don't know how to say it. A new way of thinking might help them to become unstuck and find words that will help them.

You may have also noticed that they are only exploring the topic from a limited perspective. They may have mentioned other perspectives but have not explored them. This might include taking an emotive, subjective or objective view.

You may notice aspects of their language, like links and patterns in their exploration that lend themselves to certain Emergent Coach mode interventions. They may have indicated that they want to think about the topic differently – they don't always mean this literally but I often take them at their word!

If your clients have mentioned that they paint, draw, or play music, or anything creative, they may be more open to using a creative intervention in the exploration. Don't restrict it to people who tell you they are creative, though. You might notice clients talking only in facts and logic. It's more of a stretch for them to think of using some of the more creative interventions in Emergent Coach mode, but because it is so different to their normal style, the learning can be very profound. You might have to persevere, but it is likely to be worth it.

After using Emergent Coach mode

Once you are using Emergent Coach mode successfully you will notice a range of things that are different about clients. The most obvious one is hearing a difference in what clients are saying – you can hear the change of perspective in the language they are using. Depending on the intervention used you might hear a change of context in their exploration, for example talking as if they were someone or something else in the topic. Or you might hear some of the same information being presented in a slightly different way.

You are hearing new information that clients have not mentioned before and you hear them acknowledging new information that has come into their awareness. Clients often say things like, 'I've never thought about it or looked at it this way before' or, 'It's really different looking at it like this.' They sometimes express surprise at how much information they come up with for themselves through this new exploration.

You might notice a physical change: when they start to look at something from a new perspective they often shift in their chair, sit in a different position or look towards a different part of the room. They probably have no awareness that they have moved but it gives you an indication that a shift in thinking has taken place.

The physical change may not be restricted to clients. You might find that you have also shifted position. Particularly if you are using an intervention that places the topic in the space between you, you may no longer be looking directly at the client: most of your attention will be drawn towards this space. Both of you could be observed leaning into where the topic now rests. You might also notice a different feeling in yourself. If the client was stuck you might have been feeling something related to this being stuck. If he or she has moved out of this feeling, then you are likely to notice a change of feeling too. Sometimes you might take a different role in the relationship acting as if you are an aspect of the topic, including perhaps taking the client's role in the topic.

Inadvertent use of Emergent Coach mode

The really good thing about using Emergent Coach mode is that even if you do it inadvertently it is likely to be a beneficial experience for clients. You may not have deliberately chosen this but you are encouraging them to explore the topic and access new information for themselves in a different way. Here are some of the ways that you could be using Emergent Coach mode inadvertently:

- You may find that you have some favourite interventions and there's nothing wrong in that; I think we all have them. However, if you use that intervention regularly, it might be because you enjoy using it, or out of habit. You might want to reflect on your decision-making process if you notice that you are using the same intervention regularly. You may use the same intervention because you are fairly new to coaching and have a small range of tools and techniques in your kitbag so your options are limited, in which case you might want to consider learning some new ones.

- If you have recently learnt or come across a new intervention it may be still fresh in your mind and this may be informing your choice. The intervention may fit with choosing Emergent Coach mode but it's through luck more than design. You may use it because you want to try it out rather than because it's most appropriate. If you want to try out new techniques find somewhere or someone who is willing to let you practise on them.

● There may be times when you don't have any particular views about the topic or you cannot think of anything to say, so your fall-back position is to use the first intervention that springs to mind. Potentially there's nothing wrong with this, except that it may be useful to share this with the client, as being unable to think of something to say may relate to something that is going on for the client. (I explore this in the next chapter, on Evident Coach mode.)

Risks

There are not many risks with using Emergent Coach mode predominantly compared to the other modes of presence, but you do need to bear in mind the following:

1 Colluding with the client to avoid aspects.

2 Highlighting issues that require other professional help.

3 Clients missing out on alternative learning opportunities.

1. Colluding with the client to avoid aspects

There are so many channels of perception to choose from that it is almost impossible to cover all aspects in any one session. You only have a limited amount of time available to work in. Whether you or the clients make the choices about which channels to explore you might be inadvertently colluding with them to avoid a particular aspect. Similar to the risks for Invisible Coach mode, they might be avoiding aspects of the situation, consciously or otherwise, that if explored could provide some great learning.

It's easy to avoid these aspects if you don't have time to finish the intervention in the time available. For example, if you are using objects in a constellation and you are running out of time, you might miss paying attention to one of the objects that the client has not mentioned. In this object there is something that the client finds difficult or has been avoiding. It could be the seat of the most significant learning about the topic and it's been missed. It could result in inappropriate, mediocre or flawed solutions.

2. Highlighting issues that may require other professional help

Using Emergent Coach mode the clients' exploration will expand and deepen their level of awareness. Some of this will involve accessing information that is deeper in their psyche. Some of the creative interventions can surface or provide indications of personal issues that it is not appropriate to explore in a coaching relationship. This might include an awareness or acknowledgement of a problem that could be classed as a mental health issue and the client may be best advised to seek other professional help. Depending on the issue you may be able to continue with the coaching, or it may need to cease. If you keep going with the coaching you need to keep on the coaching side of the coaching/therapy boundary. There are a too many considerations for me to cover here, but you do need to be aware of this possibility and have considered your options for an appropriate way forward should it arise. Buckley and Buckley (2006) provide a detailed guide to this aspect of coaching.

3. Clients missing out on alternative learning opportunities

In Emergent Coach mode clients do not have the opportunity to learn through the sharing of the coach's experience and/or knowledge, nor gain the insights that can be achieved through shared emotions, for example. There can be nothing wrong with this, particularly if clients have had a good learning experience, but there might be other learning that is being missed. If you have contracted to provide advice or guidance then you will need to use the two modes of presence discussed in the following chapters.

I have mentioned that this mode may surface issues that are deeper in the client's psyche, but similarly the Emergent Coach mode interventions may not go deep enough into the levels of awareness. Aspects in level four awareness often only surface through the coach directly challenging the client's thinking and as a result some of the status quo endures. Things like outdated values and limiting beliefs may not get challenged and if this is the case the client won't get the chance to overcome what is potentially the most significant barrier to moving forward. If we stay in Emergent Coach mode the opportunity for this level of learning could be lost.

Reflective questions

Think about a recent coaching session. There were probably times when you chose to be what you now might recognize as Emergent Coach mode. Identify a point when this happened.

- What happened in the lead up to you choosing this mode?

- Why did you choose to use Emergent Coach mode in that moment? What impact did this have on your client?

- Do you have a favourite technique or model, or one that you use regularly that fits with Emergent Coach mode? Think about the last time that you used this technique. What happened in the lead up to you choosing this intervention? What factors did you consider? What factors informed your decision to use this technique?

- What other options did you consider at the time? What other options might have been available to you now that you consider this in hindsight?

- Reflect on another time when you used the same model and ask yourself the same questions. What is the same about your answers? What is different about them? What does this tell you about your use of this model or technique?

- What needs to happen next for you to use Emergent Coach mode more effectively in your coaching?

Evident Coach mode

05

The key words for Evident Coach mode are:

- share;
- inform;
- prompt;
- highlight; and
- intuition.

E vident Coach mode is the third of four modes of presence for thinking about and developing your coaching presence. It's called Evident Coach mode because the client will see a higher level of input from you in the coaching relationship compared to the Invisible Coach and Emergent Coach modes. What makes it evident is that you are now sharing aspects of yourself in the coaching. There will be evidence of your contribution in the clients' exploration. In Invisible Coach and Emergent Coach modes the clients' exploration was firmly founded on their own information, their perceptions, their feelings and their opinions. In Evident Coach mode you are taking a more active role in the exploration. Clients will continue their exploration taking into account information that you have added into the mix. It is in Evident Coach mode that you are most likely to be using your intuition to aid their exploration.

Your intention in Evident Coach mode is to help clients to expand, deepen and heighten their own exploration. You are helping them to empower their own invisible coach. You want to draw aspects to their attention that will help them to either think about the topic in a different way, or pay attention to something that they have not been attending to so far. You are making it easier for them to give voice to and explore more difficult aspects of the topic. This might include helping them to surface aspects in their level three awareness and possibly aspects in their level four awareness.

Continuing the car metaphor, in Evident Coach mode you are still a passenger in the car, but now you are taking a more active role in helping the client to arrive at the destination. You are highlighting different routes on the map, pointing out places of interest, and talking about how you experienced similar places to those that you come across along the way. You talk about how the journey is making you feel and make observations about the client's choices and way of driving. The driver (the client) still decides where he or she wants to go, and which route to take, but he or she has a little more knowledge and is able to make more informed choices.

Aspects that you offer of yourself in Evident Coach mode include your feelings, emotions, words, and images, certain aspects of your experiences, knowledge and observations. When you share these you are clear why you are doing so and what you believe the impact might be – it is in the interests of the clients' learning. Clients are also clear that you are sharing something of yourself and they can choose whether to incorporate this into their exploration. I want to firmly establish here that you are not giving advice or making suggestions. The aspects that you are sharing of yourself in this mode are quite specific and do not include sharing your ideas or solutions.

You remain in Evident Coach mode long enough to share the information that you are offering to clients, then you go back to Invisible Coach mode while they continue their own exploration. You may have already started using a tool or technique in Emergent Coach mode and you may move into Evident Coach mode to deepen the exploration using the same intervention. The information that you share may be related to the exploration that has already taken place or adds new information.

When using Evident Coach mode the client remains in control of the direction of travel in the exploration. You provide the information but the client is free to decide whether to take it on board or disregard it.

Why choose Evident Coach mode

You might choose Evident Coach mode to:

1 encourage clients to talk more openly;
2 highlight aspects that clients may be missing;

3 surface unexpressed issues;

4 surface the clients' own limiters or barriers;

5 provide a fresh language with which to explore the topic;

6 inform the exploration;

7 help clients know you are on their wavelength.

1. Encourage clients to talk more openly

Sometimes when you are coaching you can get the feeling that your clients are holding back. You get a sense that they are thinking very carefully about what they share with you, perhaps not mentioning anything about their feelings. This can be the case especially at the start of the coaching relationship. They don't know you well enough yet to share some of their more personal feelings or aspects. Sharing aspects of yourself, particularly feelings or emotions, in Evident Coach mode can help the clients know that it is okay and safe to share some of the information that they might be holding back on and encourages them to talk more openly. Early on in the relationship it helps to set the scene for sharing deeper or more personal information and later on in the relationship it can be used to help them to share and explore further something that is deeper or perhaps more uncomfortable for them.

2. Highlight aspects that clients may be missing

Clients may have explored the topic from a variety of channels of perception so far but it's likely that there are aspects that they have not explored or mentioned – some they might be deliberately avoiding, others they may not be aware of. As mentioned in Emergent Coach mode, if clients don't explore the topics from some of these missing perspectives then any solutions or actions that are formulated may well be flawed. Use Evident Coach mode to encourage clients to notice and pay attention to these aspects in order to avoid flawed or mediocre solutions.

3. Surface unexpressed issues

There may be underlying issues that have yet to be surfaced that impact on the topic. If these are not addressed they will impact on the clients' ability to move forward or take action. You might not have a clear sense of what these issues are but you can see evidence of something impacting: something the client is not aware of and that without help will remain unresolved. Other times you might get a sense that the client is uncomfortable about something but is not expressing this. Some people are not comfortable acknowledging their feelings and just try to ignore them; others are very happy talking about their feelings but get uncomfortable when you invite them to talk logically about the topic.

Sharing aspects of yourself can help clients be more comfortable with some of these difficult issues and enable them to sit with the difficulty while they explore it. This may result in clients experiencing an emotional response. When this happens there is a good chance that they are close to something important in their exploration. With your help they can explore this emotional response, identify the unsurfaced issue and how it is impacting on them and find a resolution. Often what they learn about in these instances has far-reaching effects, not just for the coaching topic. Often these underlying issues are impacting in other areas of their life, and Evident Coach mode is a way of surfacing these issues for the client to gain these enabling insights. Examples of issues surfaced include learnt patterns of behaviour or triggers based on old experiences.

4. Surface the clients' own limiters or barriers

Often clients cannot move forward or find a satisfactory resolution to an issue because of a deep-rooted value or belief that is acting as a barrier and will continue to do so until it has been reframed. Some of these they may have carried with them for most of their life. They remain deep in their level four awareness. One of the reasons for using Evident Coach mode is to help clients recognize these values or beliefs and give them the opportunity to explore how valid these might be for them today. Once this has been done they can be reframed into a new belief that will serve them better going forward. An example of a belief that was impacting one of my client's was: 'I'm Italian so that makes me hot tempered and there's nothing I can do about it.'

5. Provide a fresh language with which to explore the topic

After a while it can look as if the client has run out of vocabulary to explore the topic. Clients can struggle to find ways to articulate what they mean or to understand the topic any more than they have achieved so far. Offering a new language (metaphorically speaking) with which to explore the topic can help them understand something different about it. It helps them to tap into additional information and gain insights that they might otherwise miss.

6. Inform the exploration

Rather than providing a new language with which to explore the topic, this is about providing information that could have a bearing on the exploration or any potential solutions that may come out of the coaching. No amount of exploration by clients would uncover this information because they have not come across it. It is not in any of their levels of awareness. You establish that they are not aware of this information before you offer it. Examples include new research, statistics surveys, etc.

7. Help clients know that you're on their wavelength

The quality of the relationship can have a much greater impact on the coaching outcomes than any tools and techniques used by the coach. The relationship has a bearing on the quality and depth of any learning, growth and development achieved by clients. An element of this growth comes from clients feeling validated in the relationship. They feel that they, their views and their opinions are valued and this validation helps to increase their confidence. Part of this validation comes from the fact that you understand them and are on their wavelength. You are accepting of whatever opinions or views that they might hold. When clients feel understood and validated it is easier for them to share their thinking, their difficult issues and therefore enjoy greater learning and growth. Many of the ways that you work with your clients in Evident Coach mode will communicate that you understand them, you talk the same language, you know where they are coming from, that you feel what they feel.

Beliefs

The following are some things that you might think or believe in addition to the guiding beliefs noted in the Introduction, some or all of which apply before you choose Evident Coach mode:

- I believe that clients have yet more information, data or resources within them that remain untapped, but which may be a little more difficult for them to access.
- I have information available to me that clients do not appear to have access to and that may inform their exploration or potential solutions.

- I am able to spot aspects or issues that clients may be unaware of and if surfaced will enhance their learning and growth.

- Surfacing issues or limiting beliefs and values, while difficult or uncomfortable, has the potential for a profound enabling change within the clients.

- Feelings that I experience while coaching may be related to clients or their exploration.

- My own data, whether that's feelings, experiences, knowledge, etc, when shared appropriately, may provide valuable information for clients.

How to achieve Evident Coach mode

Here are some steps you typically take when you aim to achieve Evident Coach mode:

1 Decide to use Evident Coach mode.
2 Check your motivation for sharing.
3 Tell clients what you are doing.
4 Paraphrase.
5 Let clients choose the intervention.
6 Share your own words, phrases or images.
7 Share your observations with the clients.
8 Share your factual or academic knowledge.
9 Disclose something personal about your past experiences.
10 Share new feelings and responses.
11 Share your confusion.
12 Do something novel.
13 Trust your intuition.

1. Decide to use Evident Coach mode

I know I keep saying it, but before you make any other decisions about interventions, choose the mode you are going to use. You've taken a helicopter view of the coaching relationship in the moment and you conclude that Evident Coach mode is the one that is most likely to help clients build on what they have learnt already and increase their awareness in this moment.

2. Check your motivation for sharing

As mentioned in Chapter 2 about personal factors, your motivation to share aspects of yourself may be rooted in your own interests rather than those of the clients. Take a moment before sharing to check out why exactly you are doing this. Will it genuinely serve the clients' learning? Is it possible that it is more about your desire to show how knowledgeable you are? (Insert any of the following words in place of 'knowledgeable': clever, intuitive, insightful, creative, observant, etc.) Once you know that it is in the interests of the clients' learning, go ahead. If you realize that it is something to do with your own needs, don't share. There may be times when you're not sure. It might relate to your own needs, but then again it may help the client's learning. In this case try sharing it and see what happens, but be explicit about the wariness with which you share it. It's ok to say something like: 'I'm inclined to share something with you but I'm aware it might be my own stuff but it may help with what you're talking about.' In these scenarios consider what happened in your reflective practice after the session.

3. Tell clients what you are doing

Clients may know that there will be times in the coaching when you will share something of yourself and why you might be doing this, if you have discussed it in your contracting. Sometimes clients will forget that discussion

A client was talking about taking a few minutes each day to give herself some space to think. I started to feel emotional listening to her and decided to share what I was feeling. I was certain it related to her exploration, but I didn't say that. Her reply was, 'Ah bless you!' apparently feeling sorry for me! I wondered whether I had misread this emotional response, but I was fairly sure that I hadn't. So I made it explicit. I explained that when I experienced these sensations in coaching it often related to how the client was feeling. She then acknowledged that it was feeling emotional for her: with three children and a busy full-time job she wasn't used to having any 'me time'. This resulted in a slight change in the exploration which reinforced her resolve to create this space each day for herself. Because I wasn't explicit when I shared the feeling in the first instance, it distracted the client from the exploration, but making it explicit brought her back to the exploration and to a deeper realization of the importance of her desired action.

and it may be useful when you are about to use Evident Coach mode to remind them of it. To avoid any potential confusion make it explicit that you are sharing something of yourself because you think it might have some bearing on the exploration, or that you are experiencing something and you wonder if it might relate to the topic.

4. Paraphrase

You might be wondering why I mention this here – surely you paraphrase when you reflect back in all of the modes of presence? This is not the case. In both Invisible and Emergent Coach modes you are specifically using the clients' own words when you reflect back. When paraphrasing you are making meaning of the clients' words and using your own inter-pretation to reflect back to the client what *you think* they are saying (see the Glossary for a distinction between summarizing and paraphrasing). In doing so you are giving clients an opportunity to clarify what they are thinking while also letting them know that you understand what they are saying.

When you use their exact words (as in Invisible Coach mode) there may be times when you both think that you understand each other but actually the same word carries a different meaning for each of you. Also, clients don't always use words that exactly represent what they mean. When you interpret clients' words into your own, believing these to have the same or similar meaning, clients realize if there is any misunderstanding. If the words do not work for them they will find other ways to explain what they mean. It's unlikely to require any prompting for them to explore further and clarify exactly what they do mean. If the words do work for them it can help to affirm what they are thinking, build their confidence and help them to feel that they are understood.

5. Let clients choose the intervention

If you accept the guiding beliefs in the Introduction then you believe that clients are the expert on themselves and know best what will be right for them. This includes knowing best how to continue their exploration of the topic. There are often times when you have more than one option to choose from – you can see a variety of potential lines of enquiry, or various tools or techniques that could be used. You're perhaps wondering which way to take the client now. Clients know themselves far better than you do and will have a view about what will work best for them. So free yourself from making the decision and offer the choice to the clients. Explain the interventions or lines of enquiry that you are considering and ask them how they would like to proceed. The answer may be none of those offered: the discussion might prompt an alternative or a variation.

6. Share your own words, phrases or images

Sometimes words, phrases and images will appear in your mind. It's usually clear that they relate to what clients are talking about but they are often words or images that they haven't used. When you are choosing Invisible or Emergent Coach modes you would ignore these words and images as you follow the client's own line of enquiry, but in Evident Coach mode try offering them to the client.

Before you do so it can be worth waiting a little while longer. I am often surprised to find that clients will use these same words or images without me having to mention them at all. One client was telling me about his work and the words 'born to do this' popped into my head. Within seconds he told me that he was born to do this job. If they don't use the words or images and you think it might add something to the exploration then go ahead and share them. When you do choose to offer the words or image, preface the intervention with something that makes it clear that these are your own words or images, for example: 'When you said that this image/ these words popped into my head...'. Often when you share an image you find that the client chooses to use the image to continue the exploration of the topic.

The images may not only be restricted to objects or other people: images might be of yourself, of you doing something in response to what the client is talking about, for example giving someone a hug or slapping someone, or running away, or handing over an award. You might find that these images reflect something the client feels like doing but is not acknowledging at the moment. Offering these images can sometimes help the client to voice something that he or she has not felt it appropriate to voice so far.

Sometimes it's worth thinking about a metaphor for clients to use as a means of exploring the topic. In Emergent Coach mode you may use a metaphor that they have used already. In Evident Coach mode you think of an appropriate metaphor for them to use to explore the topic. You use your own knowledge and experience to form views about what perspectives they need to consider and choose a metaphor that will help them to explore this.

I was working with a client who had high hopes for promotion for one of his team members but was getting frustrated because she wasn't completing any of the actions agreed. Knowing what I know about developing people and the way people learn and grow, my view was that it sounded like some important groundwork was missing. Based on my experience I knew that this was an important factor so I chose to use Evident Coach mode to help him to work this out for himself. I decided to offer him a metaphor that would help him to consider the groundwork needed. I was explicit and told him that I was going to invite him to think about this in a different way and requested that he trust me and give this a go.

I asked him to describe what he would do if he was a farmer who wanted to produce a crop from a currently fallow field. Through this discussion he talked about reading up and learning about what crops could be harvested, finding out as much information as he could about the options, including what income he could earn and what other benefits there could be from growing these crops; testing the soil to see what type it was and learning about how to prepare the soil so that the crops could grow ie fertilize the soil with particular types of nutrients.

Following this I asked him how this all correlated with the person he had high hopes for. He acknowledged that he didn't know if she even really wanted a promotion. He guessed that she did not really understand the options open to her or how she might benefit from them. He realized that this might be why she was quite hesitant and wasn't carrying out the agreed actions. There were a range of possible promotions open to her which were quite different and would need different types of development. One of his first steps was to help her to find out more about her options and help her to work out what she wanted. He still hoped that she would progress. Armed with this new awareness he also realized that her choice of role would inform the skills that she would need to develop so they would need to identify these and then draw up a development plan tailored to what she wanted to achieve. This became another of his action steps.

The client had all this information within him, and exploring the situation through the metaphor he gained a deeper understanding of not just what to do but also why he needed to change his approach with his team member.

7. Share your observations with the client

As you are paying attention to your clients you notice and make a note of all sorts of aspect in their exploration – patterns of words or behaviour, changes in their physicality, an emphasis on certain words, beliefs that might be getting in their way, assumptions, comparisons, generalizations and so on (see Caulfield, 2012 and Charvet, 1997 for more on how people use language). Much of this goes on outside of the clients' awareness and when brought to their attention can be useful data and lead to them gaining new insights. Share some of the aspects that you have noticed.

8. Share your factual or academic knowledge

When clients are talking about their topic you may have knowledge that they have not come across and that might help them in their exploration. This information might impact on the topic or potential solutions. Alternatively you may have information that offers them an alternative way of thinking about the topic. In Evident Coach mode this does not include your views or opinions. Examples include new research, the latest figures, a recent survey, work that is happening in another department, an academic model or a business tool. Before you offer the information check out what they know already. I find it quite embarrassing to launch into the detail of some information only to find that the client knows about it (and often knows it better than I do!) When the knowledge shared impacts on the topic or has a direct link, simply introduce it by asking if they are aware of it.

When you want to share knowledge that will help them to explore the topic in a different way this will usually be triggered by or relate to language they are using. Here's an example: when clients are describing conflict situations they often use words like 'victimized' or 'persecuted', or they talk about someone 'acting like a child' or say something like, 'He thinks he's my Dad!' For me the first words trigger thoughts about the drama triangle. The second pair of words triggers thoughts of ego states. Both are models from transactional analysis (Stewart and Joines, 1987) and both can be a helpful way of exploring what's happening in a conflict situation. Make sure that whatever you offer is congruent with the language they have used.

In this example if I decide to share my knowledge of either of these models it would be incongruent if I talked about ego states for the first example and the drama triangle for the second. They are already using similar language in relation to the situation, so offering the information provides them with a more structured way of using the same language. It can also help them to work out how to change their behaviour using the same language. You are not teaching them the models. If they want to know more about the models you can point them towards other resources for further learning.

I was coaching someone to develop his presentation skills in readiness for his first presentation to a large group. I could see evidence that his nerves might be getting in the way, but they were not being mentioned. So I talked about my first experience of standing up and doing a presentation to a large group. I talked about being so scared that I could barely speak, I couldn't remember what I wanted to say and I couldn't read my notes because I'd lost my place and in my panic I couldn't find it again. The client immediately started talking about his fears about what happens to him when he gets nervous. As a result we were able to work out some strategies to help him deal with the nerves when he had to do his presentation.

9. Disclose something personal about your past experiences

Have you ever noticed that when you disclose how you are feeling, or disclose some personal information about yourself, the person you are talking to opens up and shares something personal about him or herself? When you've shared something it somehow makes it easier for the other person to do the same.

You can use this phenomenon to great effect when coaching. You may feel that there is something unspoken or unaddressed in the exploration. It might be that clients are holding back in their exploration, or they are avoiding talking about their feelings, or there are assumptions clouding the issue. You may have your own experiences to draw on. Use these to help clients surface the aspects they are currently avoiding. You are talking about what was happening at the time for you, not what you did. Don't mix this up with making suggestions. You share your feelings, thoughts or assumptions deliberately to enable clients to talk about aspects they might be holding back on. You share what you felt, or thought, at the time. State that you are talking about your own experience. Tell clients what happened and what your worries, concerns or feelings were. When clients hear you talking about these aspects there is a good chance that they relate to it and open up about their feelings.

10. Share new feelings and responses

The previous section was about sharing feelings and information about your past experiences. Now I am talking about sharing emotions, feelings and data that are experienced in the moment during the coaching. Just as images or words pop into our heads while working with clients, so do new emotions, sensations and feelings, and these can provide really useful data for clients or their topic. When these show up they often originate from our clients. We start to feel things physically that are a reflection of what they may be feeling. If you suddenly feel your eyes getting heavy, or butterflies in your tummy, or you notice yourself clenching your teeth, tapping your foot, starting to feel angry or upset, or whatever new sensation you become aware of, share this with the client. (For further information about this refer to mode six of the seven-eyed model; Hawkins and Shohet, 2012.) Bringing this data to their attention can help clients acknowledge or notice something that they may be missing or avoiding and this can then be used to inform their exploration of the topic.

This is why it is important to know yourself and how you are feeling before the start of a session. If you have prepared yourself as outlined in Chapter 1, you will recognize quickly when you start to experience feelings or activity within yourself that might be linked to the relationship with the client.

11. Share your confusion

Although this comes under the heading of sharing your responses, I mention it separately as you may feel confused when clients are talking about a topic because of the language they are using. Before sharing your confusion check out its potential source. Is it obvious that the clients know what they are talking about? Perhaps it's just the company jargon or type of language they are using that you do not understand. If they are using jargon or language that you are not used to and they are clearly not confused, let them carry on. However, if this is not the case then your confusion may be reflecting how they are feeling, and it may be worth sharing and asking for clarification. The question to ask in this scenario is, 'Will asking them to clarify add anything to their exploration?' Often asking them to explain the jargon or language can be just addressing your need for clarity, rather than helping their exploration.

12. Do something novel

Every so often you get inspired. You are in the flow (Csikszentmihalyi, 1990; 2004). Everything is going really well. Suddenly you have an instinct to do something different to anything you've done before. It seems to have come out of nowhere but in the moment you have a strong belief that it is the right thing to do. Your instincts tell you that there is something significant here, and this new idea will help the client to break through this significant element. But there's another voice in your head saying, 'Oh no, be careful. You've not done this before. What if it doesn't work? What happens if you get it wrong? What will the client think? No – it's too wacky!' (Wacky can be great, believe me!) The idea is different, unfamiliar, and sometimes comes with a bit of fear attached to it. If it's risky from a health and safety perspective, then pause for thought (I have no idea what this wacky idea might be, remember!) If the health and safety aspect is ok, then go for it. Offer your novel approach to the client. Then reflect on what happened in your reflective practice.

13. Trust your intuition

Sharing emotions, feelings or sensations that we notice in ourselves in the coaching can feel risky, particularly if you are not used to doing this with your clients, and it can be hard to be sure that you have differentiated between data that is related to you and data that is related to the client, or the client relationship. My advice here is: trust your intuition and go with it. You may not know where it will lead but there's a good chance that it can open up a client's thinking. It might not always go smoothly. But even when it doesn't go quite as you expected it can open up a new avenue of exploration.

For a long time I didn't trust my intuition: I would share what I was feeling but I often got it wrong. Then I learnt to share the feelings or emotions, without interpretation or attaching some meaning to them, and now I mostly get it right. The intuition was right, it was the labels I was using that were wrong.

Take the risk – possibly one of the most important points for Evident Coach mode. Many times when I have done something new with my clients it has felt quite risky. My heart has been in my mouth. The first time I got someone to draw a picture, or got someone out of their chair moving around, the first time I used chair work, etc – often these came from my intuition and not my learning. Often the feedback from my clients has been that these were pivotal moments in the coaching. I always reflect on these after the session and these instances often highlight and open up new avenues for my learning journey.

Trust your intuition. Be prepared to try things and get it wrong. Remember that clients can always choose not to use it if it doesn't feel right for them.

Things you may notice

Before using Evident Coach mode

You have noticed how clients have used particular types of words, perhaps patterns to their words. You have noticed links in what they are talking about now to other aspects mentioned, or you have noticed changes in their physicality. And you wonder what these things might be about or whether they are aware of the connection or change.

You notice a change in yourself. You are suddenly experiencing something physically or emotionally that you were not aware of previously. These are thoughts and feelings that you believe are not related to your own personal matters. You wonder if they are anything to do with the client or their exploration.

In Emergent Coach mode you have offered clients different interventions designed to help them to consider alternative channels of perception, but their exploration remains limited to certain aspects and you are aware of other channels that they seem to be missing. The client is talking in very factual, logical terms and not mentioning anything related to feelings or emotions, or vice versa.

You realize that you are aware of some factual information that might be relevant to the topic. The client seems to be unaware of this as he or she has not mentioned it.

The client is talking about something you have experienced personally. You remember your thoughts and feelings about this and there may be hints of these in the client's exploration that he or she has not expressed.

He or she is using language that is used in certain models or academic information and these can be applied in the context that the client is discussing. The client has not mentioned the model or the information and you believe that some knowledge of this might help him or her to explore the topic in a slightly different way.

After using Evident Coach mode

You will know you have been successful in using mode three when you see changes in the clients' exploration. Clients pick up what you have shared with them and use it as a way of continuing their exploration. They may ask questions about what you have shared but these are likely to be for clarification only. You can hear evidence of what you have shared in their continued exploration, or their exploration moves into an area that they appeared to be previously missing or avoiding. In the conflict example mentioned earlier, clients start to talk about the drama triangle or ego states to continue their exploration.

You may see some emotions arise in clients that you were not seeing before. The sharing of feelings or emotions in particular can trigger an emotional response in clients. They are now exploring this aspect where this was previously avoided. Or you may see more analytical or logical thinking where previously only feelings were being explored.

As with Emergent Coach mode, sometimes you will see a change in their posture: they have heard something that has changed their way of thinking and you see the shift in the thinking reflected in a shift in their body language. Sometimes they move, change position and look in a different direction.

Inadvertent use of Evident Coach mode

People will use something like Evident Coach mode in everyday interactions automatically. It's natural to share our thoughts, experiences and knowledge, and to talk about our feelings to another person. Often it's done for no other purpose than to have an enjoyable social interaction. This way of interacting with others will show up in our coaching because it feels natural to do so. However, when coaching we need to think more consciously about what we are sharing and why we are sharing it. It is only shared in the interests of the client's learning. If you do it automatically without considering why you are doing it, this is inadvertent use of Evident Coach mode.

I know I keep saying it, but here's another reminder that just because you do it inadvertently doesn't make it right or wrong. But we can learn a lot from noticing when we do it inadvertently to become more competent at using it consciously.

Sharing aspects of ourselves may be more to do with our own needs than it is in the interest of the client's learning. Sometimes we share our own thoughts, views and experiences to make ourselves feel good – we have a burning desire to show that we know stuff! Or maybe we want to make a good impression so that the clients continue working with us (and continue paying our fee). We try to impress them with our expertise. In the moment we don't always realize that this is what we are doing and it is inadvertent Evident Coach mode.

Often coaches will use their own words and phrases, thoughts or images without being explicit about it to the client. Sometimes in Evident Coach mode you will choose not to be explicit about it but you will be aware of what you are doing. If you are using Evident Coach mode without being explicit there's a greater chance that you have done so without thinking about why you are doing it and what impact it might have on the client.

If you regularly share your own knowledge or previous experiences in coaching, albeit different every time, then this is possibly inadvertent use of Evident Coach mode. Often what the clients talk about will trigger memories of times when you have had similar experiences and you may almost always share these memories. Sharing your knowledge or previous experience is something you will do sporadically as an intervention. If you are doing it regularly, for example at least once in every coaching session, you might want to reflect on what is informing this as an intervention.

Are you regularly sharing the same knowledge with a number of different clients? I know I have a couple of models that I share quite often, and can sometimes find myself tempted to share these same models when actually the client has not provided any triggers for them. Sharing the same information regularly does not make it wrong – you may be working with a number of clients for whom this is useful information – but you do need to check why you consider this to be useful for this particular client.

How often do you continue while being confused? If the answer is never, you always seek clarification, then you are probably using Evident Coach mode inadvertently. The outcome may be that it helps clients with their exploration, but similarly it may just interrupt their flow because they know what they are talking about and explaining it to you does not add anything. Expect to be confused sometimes in your coaching.

Risks

As with all the modes of presence there are upsides and downsides; here are the risks associated with Evident Coach mode:

1 Clients choose to reject the data.
2 Surface powerful emotions.
3 Coach bias.
4 Inadvertently limit client options.
5 Embarrassed coach.
6 Clients misread your intention.

1. Clients choose to reject the data

In any of the modes of presence, clients have a choice. In Evident Coach mode they decide what they do with any information that has been shared; this includes rejecting any information that you might share. Your first thought may be that this rejection says something about the value of what you have shared, but it is not always the case. Remember, sometimes what you share is aimed at surfacing something that might be quite difficult for the client so it may not get accepted first time around. It may be to do with the client's readiness to consider this aspect. If your sharing does seem to get rejected, it is useful to consider what happened in your reflective practice.

2. Surface powerful emotions

In Evident Coach mode sometimes you are intentionally bringing feelings and emotions into play and as a result may elicit a strong emotional response in the client. Once surfaced these emotions might be quite difficult to deal with for both of you. Once they have been surfaced, it can be a bit like Pandora's Box – once the lid has been lifted you can't push the contents back in. It is unlikely that the client will be able to explore any other aspect once these have been surfaced. You need to remain grounded so that you are not drawn into the emotion, while the client sits with the emotion to access the learning that may be derived from the experience. When you help the client to explore these strong emotions you need to keep it in the context of the coaching topic and on the right side of the coaching/therapy boundary, or you need to recognize when it might require other professional help (see Buckley and Buckley, 2006).

3. Coach bias

In Chapter 2 I talked about hooks as a personal factor that may influence your coaching. When sharing something of yourself, particularly when you are making observations or replaying information back to the client, you are being selective about what data to use. This is where these hooks may be coming into play. Coaches may believe that they are replaying information that appears to have some emphasis or weight for the client, but the resonance may be coming from the coach and not the client. The coach is hearing emphasis on information or data because it reflects something that he or she is wrangling with.

4. Inadvertently limit client options

When using Evident Coach mode you will sometimes present options. The client may perceive that these are the only options available and this inadvertently closes down other routes. Avoid this by making it clear that there are always other alternatives, even if they have not been mentioned.

5. Embarrassed coach

When we do something completely new, either to us or the client, we often worry that it's going to fall flat. And there is the chance that it might not work out the way that we thought it would, especially if we are trying something novel or following our intuition, and that might feel embarrassing. But don't worry about it – it's okay! Clients may be resistant to the idea at first: it might be taking them out of their comfort zone and they are not yet ready for this. When this happens it can offer you a new way of exploring the topic with them. The intervention may not be the issue: it could be what it's likely to surface that is causing the resistance, so you can explore their resistance to the intervention. What is it about the idea that doesn't feel right, or that they don't like? How does that relate to the topic? Talking about the intervention without doing it can provide clients with a different way of exploring the topic, and they may even go with it later.

6. Clients misread your intention

Occasionally when you share something of yourself, particular factual or academic information, clients can read this as an opportunity to ask for advice or suggestions. This can be linked to how explicit the coach was about what he or she was doing. Don't get drawn into giving advice or suggestions until you are sure that the time is right for the clients' learning.

Reflective questions

- Next time you find yourself replaying information back to the client notice the words you are using. Whose words are they? Are you paraphrasing or summarizing? (See the distinction in Glossary.)

- Keep a record of times when you share your knowledge or experience, including what it was you shared. How often are you sharing your knowledge or experiences? What patterns emerge about the frequency or the type of knowledge or experience you are sharing? What is this telling you about your use of Evident Coach mode?

- Reflect on a recent time when you shared your knowledge or experience. What happened in the lead up to you doing this? What were the triggers that led you to share this with the client? What did the client do with the information? What other options were open to you that you now recognize in hindsight? What does the answer to these questions tell you about your sharing of yourself? What, if anything, will you do differently next time?

- Reflect on a time when you have introduced your own thinking into the coaching. How did you introduce this into the session?

- Think about a time when you have experienced an emotional response while coaching. If this response was related to you, what might this be attributed to? If the emotional response was related to the client, what might it be attributed to? What did you do with the data you received in the coaching session? What might you have done differently? What might have been the impact of this?

- Still thinking about your recent coaching, identify an Evident Coach mode experience when you went with your instincts and tried something completely new. What happened in the lead up to this? What were you noticing in the client that led you to the intervention? What happened? Why do you think this happened?

- Based on this experience, how will you know next time that this intervention might be appropriate? What would you do differently to make the intervention more successful if you were to do it again? What learning would help you to use this type of intervention more proficiently in the future? If you did not go ahead with the intervention because the client was resistant to the idea, consider what this might have been about for the client.

Visible Coach mode

06

The key words for Visible Coach mode are:

- steer;
- direct;
- incite;
- probe;
- challenge;
- provoke; and
- courage.

This is the fourth of the four modes of presence. It's Visible Coach mode because your presence is more overt than in any of the other modes: you are steering the coaching session in some way. It is unlikely (although not out of the question) that you would start in Visible Coach mode; it is more likely that you will have worked your way through at least one or two of the other modes of presence before you decide to engage in Visible Coach mode. The four modes of presence can be seen as progressive, with Visible Coach mode often being the final choice. It builds on and enhances the learning that has been achieved in the previous modes.

Your intention in Visible Coach mode is to incite a response in clients. You want to help them to access information that is in their level four awareness, so that they can achieve more profound learning, which can be transformational in nature and has the potential to impact on their whole life, and not just their working life (or the aspect you are focused on). Your intention may be to take them out of their comfort zone, because you know that this is where the potential for transformational learning can lie.

Your coaching expertise tells you that something is happening that would be beneficial for the client to explore. You have views based on your experience and relating to how clients are exploring the topic. Sometimes you are making judgements about what you think may be happening for them. All of this influences your choice of interventions in Visible Coach mode.

You press clients more in this mode than in any other mode of presence, particularly when they appear to be avoiding certain aspects or interventions. Ultimately clients can decline the invitation to explore the suggested route but not without a little persistence from you first. You won't force them, but you will push them to go further with their exploration than perhaps they would do without this pressure. Sometimes all clients need is a little adjustment time, some encouragement and some reassurance before using an intervention or exploring something that they perceive to be quite difficult. You provide support while making it just a little harder for them to dodge or evade the perspective.

When you use Visible Coach mode to steer the direction of travel you may need strong resolve. You need to have the courage of your convictions to keep going with the intervention. Clients may not be comfortable or indeed happy with the intervention or direction of travel you are steering them towards. It might be uncomfortable for you too and it could make your life a lot easier if you were to just let it go. But you know that these interventions have the potential to make a profound difference: clients would miss out on some great learning if you cave in at the first sign of resistance and let them choose not to go there. There will be times when you have to hold your nerve when using Visible Coach mode.

In Visible Coach mode you may be using some of the same tools and techniques as in previous modes, but *how* you use the intervention changes. You start being more directive about how clients use the tool or technique to continue in their exploration.

Like Emergent and Evident Coach modes, you do not stay in Visible Coach mode for long. Once the client is going ahead with the intervention you go back into Invisible Coach mode offering time and space while the client explores this avenue. However, you may find that you need to shift more frequently between Invisible Coach and Visible Coach modes as you help the client to continue with this direction of travel. There is potentially a higher level of coach input using Visible Coach mode than any of the other modes of presence.

Going back to the car metaphor, in Visible Coach mode you are still a passenger. This time you are reading the map and giving the driver directions. You are quite insistent that the driver follows the route you are suggesting because you know that there is something interesting to see if this route is taken, or it may help in getting to the destination quicker by working around stop signs, barriers and diversions that would normally prevent the driver reaching the destination. However, the driver has control of the car and ultimately he or she decides which way to drive.

Why choose Visible Coach mode

You might choose Visible Coach mode to:

1 facilitate a shift in clients;
2 incite new thinking;
3 enable a greater/deeper level of learning;
4 open up new options for clients;
5 keep it a coaching relationship;
6 challenge illegal, dangerous or unethical behaviour.

1. Facilitate a shift in clients

If clients are to achieve transformational learning, a shift is often required (Hawkins and Shohet, 2012) – something fundamental needs to move or change. Examples include: changing the way they are thinking (for example focusing on the positive rather than the negative), a reframing of a limiting belief, seeing an assumption for what it is, addressing a deep-rooted issue, moving beyond an irrational fear, making a decision, etc. When these shifts happen you can see the change in the client in the room, and when this happens there is a much greater chance that the change will translate into new behaviours or thinking outside of the coaching relationship. If you have been working in the previous modes of presence, you may have seen clients moving about or shifting position as what or how their thinking has been changing. This is different. When there is a fundamental shift in clients you see it in their being. You hear and see a new energy; the pace, tone and pitch of their voice changes. Their whole body changes, you see differences in the level of movement, gesticulation, posture. You can physically see and hear the difference.

The first shift you might facilitate is when clients first arrive. This is covered in Chapter 1, when I discussed facilitating clients' presence. You deliberately steer the conversation until they are in a calm, quiet and relaxed state from which they are able to access their own invisible coach within them. Towards the end of a session you might steer clients to rehearse an action so that they are prepared for when they have to do it for real. Both of these are Visible Coach mode in action. In between the two you are likely to be facilitating a change in something more deep-rooted and will probably need a little more help and encouragement to bring it about.

2. Incite new thinking

You may use Visible Coach mode to help clients see how their outdated ways of thinking are holding them back. They may be holding on to longstanding values and beliefs that no longer serve them well. Values and beliefs that are so deeply rooted clients don't notice their existence. You may have tried to highlight them through other modes but clients do not see them. To move forward they need to explore these and check out whether they remain valid, and if not work out what they are going to believe that is different. You may need to press them to achieve this, and Visible Coach mode can be used to help clients reconsider old values, beliefs and assumptions and to reframe them so that they can move forward.

3. Enable a greater/deeper level of learning

If we are going to help our clients to actualize their full potential (Maslow, 1943) we need to help them access greater depths of learning. This learning cannot be achieved in the safety of their comfort zone. They already know what is inside their comfort zone and work done inside the comfort zone is potentially affirmation or confirmation of existing knowledge that may help with confidence building and so has its place. However, transformational growth and development comes through expanding their comfort zone. At some point clients need to explore the area that is outside of the comfort zone: this is where the really rich learning takes place. But they may be quite resistant to exploring this so may need your help to do so. Once they have explored and become familiar with aspects outside of the comfort zone, the zone expands to encompass the new learning.

4. Open up new options for clients

Exploring the topic through a wide variety of lenses and channels of perception will automatically help clients see new options as a result. Each new channel brings a different understanding that has the potential to provide clients with options they had previously not considered. Pressing them to explore aspects they have been avoiding or find difficult will often generate new and significant insights, which in turn opens up avenues that they may not have known existed. Helping clients to reframe old thinking habits may help them open doors that were closed to them previously, unaware that they were the ones holding the door closed.

5. Keep it a coaching relationship

Sometimes in the coaching relationship aspects will arise that are better dealt with by others. There will be times when clients are best served by seeking other types of professional help. This may be because the area they need help with requires more knowledge-based learning, for example marketing or project management, or because there are mental health issues that need resolving. However, clients may think otherwise – you have helped them so much already that they believe that you can help them with anything. They may try to press you to keep on working with them on these new topics, which may result in this moving from a coaching relationship to something else, perhaps consultancy, an advisory role or therapy.

In particular there can be quite a blurred line between coaching and therapy. Sometimes the work we do can be perceived as therapeutic by clients. The opportunity to have someone listen and pay attention to them for an hour or so can be quite cathartic. If you believe that continuing with a particular client will result in the relationship moving to something other than coaching you may need to use Visible Coach mode to steer the client's exploration so that he or she recognizes this.

Some coaches will have the background and the skills to deal with some of these new aspects that the client wants help with. The question then is, 'What are you contracted to provide?'

6. *Challenge illegal, dangerous or unethical behaviour*

There are some aspects that may come up in a coaching relationship that you have a legal, moral, ethical or contractual obligation to explore. It's likely to be a rare occurrence but there may be occasions that require you to break client confidentiality and report activity to the company or appropriate authorities. Before you take this course of action I suggest that you need to explore the situation fully with the client first. This is where you may need to hold onto the courage of your convictions. When potentially illegal, dangerous or unethical ideas are mentioned as realistic options you move into Visible Coach mode and steer the exploration to challenge these actions (or proposed actions) and help him or her to reconsider, draw different conclusions and find more ethical, safe or legal alternatives.

Challenging these can be quite a difficult conversation to have, made even more difficult if you did not discuss these as possible eventualities at the outset (see contracting). And if you do find yourself in a position like this, I recommend that you discuss it with a qualified coaching supervisor (see Chapter 8).

Beliefs

Here are some beliefs that are specific to using Visible Coach mode:

- Transformational learning can take place in the clients' discomfort zone. They have the potential to learn something profound when they are exploring something that might be uncomfortable or difficult for them.
- I am willing to risk inciting an emotional response in clients in the interest of their learning.
- Focusing clients' attention on their blind or deaf spots has the potential to uncover some deeper learning and greater growth potential.
- Factors relating to the clients' topic, issues or relationships can surface in the way that I work with my clients and can provide useful data to inform the exploration.
- Transformational learning has not taken place until I see evidence of the shift in the room.
- I am obliged to challenge clients if what they are proposing is unethical, illegal or represents a danger to either themselves or another.

How to achieve Visible Coach mode

The following is a list of ways in which you can achieve Visible Coach mode followed by a little more detail about each:

1 Decide to use Visible Coach mode.

2 Be courageous.

3 Interrupt clients' flow.

4 Offer an opposite viewpoint.

5 Repeat the intervention.

6 Ease clients into their discomfort zone.

7 Change how you use the intervention.

8 Focus on the assumption or belief behind the thinking.

9 Steer clients towards the cause of the emotion.

10 Explore the parallel process.

11 Challenge and explore ethical issues.

12 Suggest potential solutions.

13 Manage the coaching process.

1. Decide to use Visible Coach mode

If you have already read about the other three modes then you know what this is! Before choosing any intervention you make a deliberate decision to choose the mode. The choice of intervention or how you use the intervention is determined by the mode.

2. Be courageous

One of the key words for Visible Coach mode is 'courage'. You are encouraging clients to handle some potentially difficult aspects. You need to provide them with an environment where it is safe and secure for them to do so. If you are worried or concerned (or scared even) they will sense that in you and it will not feel safe for them.

You may find some of the aspects personally challenging. It's not always easy to do. Many people choose to avoid any type of conflict or confrontation, which is what this challenge may feel like at times. It will sometimes take courage to challenge the client. To be courageous it will help if your intentions are securely grounded in the interest of the clients' learning and you are clear about the reasons you are taking this stand in the relationship. When you have both of these you can be confident in your requests, and clients are likely to feel safe enough to go ahead.

3. Interrupt clients' flow

Most of us were brought up to believe that we should not interrupt others when they are speaking; we patiently wait for an opening to speak. But when you do this, clients can follow a line of thinking that is familiar, comfortable and which leads them to the same old conclusions and nothing new is learnt. Behaviours stay the same and they don't achieve the outcomes they are looking for. You intervene to prevent clients from following an old familiar way of thinking and to incite fresh thinking, different conclusions and new learning. One way of doing this is to interrupt their thinking. Stop them in their tracks. Don't even let them finish their sentence. Stop them before they settle into their comfort zone. Stop them and steer their thinking towards new channels of perception.

4. Offer an opposite viewpoint

You might try offering clients an opposite or contrary view to those they are expressing. This can have the effect of cementing their conclusions as they defend their position against the contrary view or opening up questions or doubts in their thinking. The view expressed does not have to be one that you believe or agree with. In Visible Coach mode remember that you are not imposing your own views on clients: this is just another channel for them to consider before they finally draw their own conclusions or formalize their actions.

An opposite view may include the way that they explore the topic. Some people will talk about a particular aspect in a quite detached, objective way; others may talk about it more subjectively. Encourage clients to explore the topic in a more objective or subjective way. Encourage them to explore the facts of the topic, or how people concerned might feel about it, whichever is opposite to how they normally talk. It can be quite uncomfortable for them to explore the topic in an opposite way but it gets them using their brain differently to how they are used to using it and therefore they start to think differently.

5. Repeat the intervention

You've asked a question, made an observation, offered a technique and your clients have ignored it. They have chosen to take the exploration in a different direction. Perhaps they've answered a different question to the one asked or chosen not to use the technique offered. In all the other modes of presence this is ok – clients choose whether to accept your intervention or not. But you offered this particular intervention for a very good reason. You've probably invited them to explore something that they might find uncomfortable, so it's not surprising that they might dodge or evade it for a while. In Visible Coach mode we don't let them dodge it quite so easily! So offer the intervention again to see if they pick it up.

6. Ease clients into their discomfort zone

In Visible Coach mode you are pushing your clients towards exploring something that is uncomfortable, so it's natural for them to want to avoid this if they can. Sometimes we need to allow clients some time and space to get used to the idea of moving into their discomfort zone. If someone was learning to abseil, you wouldn't just push them over the edge (I hope!) – you would give them some gentle encouragement and wait patiently while they got used to the height, found their feet and tested the harnesses so that eventually they felt ready to go. For some people, without a little pressure they would give up and never feel the sense of satisfaction that comes from abseiling to the bottom. But press them too hard and they dig their heels in and refuse to do it. Some take longer than others, and require more encouragement. A few will never do it, no matter how much encouragement they get. The same applies to coaching people into their discomfort zone.

One way of easing someone into their discomfort zone is to continue in Visible Coach mode by steering towards a discussion about the intervention rather than the topic. Once you have discussed this you can agree a way forward that will often (but not always) include going back to the intervention. Doing this first can give clients time to prepare themselves to face the difficult aspect. As you get to know your clients you get a feel for how much you can press them while they still feel safe.

I invited a client to consider the topic from another person's point of view by adopting the posture of the other person. I recognized that this might be uncomfortable for her. In response, she started talking about something else. My sense was that she needed some time to adjust to the idea so I dropped back into Invisible Coach mode and listened to her while she digressed. After a short while I said to her in a light-hearted tone, 'Have you digressed for long enough yet? Are you ready to do this yet?' At this point she laughed and said yes, and then explored the more difficult situation from the other person's point of view. The exploration surfaced an underlying assumption about the other person that wasn't true and which changed her view of him. This changed her attitude about him and suddenly the problem dissolved.

In this case it wasn't that she wasn't prepared to try the intervention, she just wasn't quite ready to do so. If I had remained in one of the other modes of presence and allowed her to continue in her own direction of travel, she might not have explored this. If I had pressed her immediately she might have felt that her safety was in question, and she might still have refused. Allowing her the time and space to digress gave her a chance to get comfortable with the idea and eased her into her discomfort zone. Asking her if she was ready to do so also put the exploration under her control (she could have said no).

7. Change how you use the intervention

As I mentioned in the Introduction, the mode you choose determines how you use an intervention. Most interventions lend themselves to be used in a variety of modes of presence. (In Chapter 7 there are examples of how the way you work with interventions changes in the different modes of presence.) You may start using an intervention in Emergent or Evident Coach modes and you continue using this from Visible Coach mode, but now you start steering clients towards aspects of the intervention. You make observations and ask questions specifically about areas they are avoiding. If for example they are using a drawing to explore the issue, you make observations or ask questions about specific things that you notice in the drawing, for example, 'That group of people is a long way from this group of people' or, 'Why is that symbol higher on the page than this symbol?'

8. Focus on the assumption or belief behind the thinking

While clients are exploring the topic it can be easier for you to notice when assumptions or beliefs may be getting in their way. You can see them informing the clients' view. When you notice these, bring them to the clients' attention and encourage them to explore the assumption or belief. Encourage them to consider what is stopping them from going forward and whether this still hold true for them now that they've considered it. Sometimes it's not enough just to realize it logically – it needs to be felt too. Steer clients to keep this in focus until they have reframed the assumption or belief.

In the case study below I could see that a shift in the room had not happened, even though the client appeared to have recognized what was behind her thinking. I used repetition and perseverance until she found a way to reframe this. This was a deep-rooted and difficult issue for the client and she was in her discomfort zone exploring it. The focus of attention was firmly rooted in the limiting belief that was holding her back. I knew when she had finally reframed this by observing the shift in her.

I worked with a client who was going through a bit of a confidence crisis. This was the topic that she wanted to explore that day. I started in Invisible Coach mode and gave her time and space to talk about the topic. She talked of being self-employed and the main breadwinner in the family, the recession and the fact that her income was substantially lower than she had been used to. As we progressed through the session I noticed what appeared to be a link between her level of confidence and income levels. I encouraged her to consider this aspect and it transpired that she measured her self-worth by how much income she earned. Her confidence was linked to her sense of self-worth. Low income meant low worth and therefore her confidence was low. I encouraged her to explore this belief and she got it – intellectually. Logically it did not make any sense but it wasn't really making any difference. I had not seen the shift in the client. So I encouraged her to consider times in her life when there was no money involved but she really believed in herself. It took three repeats of the intervention before she was able to find an example but finally she came up with a very powerful example in her private life, when she absolutely believed in herself and there was no money involved. We explored that time in some detail and she was able to reframe the criteria for her own self-belief so it no longer depended on her income levels. The belief was no longer true for her and the difference in her was palpable. The shift in the room was obvious. Her whole demeanour changed. She beamed and her eyes lit up. Her body posture straightened; she looked as if she was lighter all of a sudden.

9. *Steer clients towards the cause of the emotion*

When someone gets angry or upset a common reaction in others is to try to calm the person down or get them to stop crying. The first instinct is to rescue the person by trying to curb the emotion that has just surfaced. In coaching, when clients respond emotionally this can be a really good sign – they are potentially on the edge of powerful learning as long as the coach refrains from rescuing and grounds him or herself so that he or she is not drawn into the emotion. Remain detached and help clients sit with the emotion. Hold onto your empathy and the fact that you are doing this in the interest of their learning. This will help you to remain detached. You can then steer clients to

A client I was working with had a very emotional response. She had difficulty handling team members who challenged her and this was the topic we were exploring. I had been using Invisible and Emergent Coach modes and the client was exploring the topic quite calmly. Suddenly she started crying. She was remembering a traumatic experience that had happened in her childhood. Knowing that there was the potential for some profound learning I steered the exploration through the emotion. I invited her to tell me about it. She recounted the story and told me that at the time she felt badly let down by the authorities. She was still crying as she was talking about it. It had obviously been a significant event in her life. To keep the discussion grounded in coaching I asked her how this story related to the topic that we were discussing. She said that she felt powerless when anyone challenged her. Her mind would go blank and she couldn't think what to say or do. She was still showing some signs of emotional distress but she was containing this and was able to talk through it. We explored the topic further and she acknowledged that it was the childhood experience that was impacting on her ability to handle challenges now, particularly if there was an element of aggression or assertiveness in the other person.

She went on to develop some strategies to help her deal with team members in the moment that gave her time to think, compose herself and decide what to do. If I had tried to rescue her she might never have realized how this childhood experience was impacting on her still. Any solutions would not have taken this into account and therefore it would have been unlikely she would have achieved her desired outcome.

explore what has arisen. What has caused the emotional response, and how is it relevant to the topic that they are currently exploring?

10. *Explore the parallel process*

In Visible Coach mode you pay attention to what Hawkins and Smith (2006) refer to as the 'parallel process'. It can often be the case that aspects of how clients work with other people, or what clients want to be different when working with other people, will show up in your coaching relationship. This usually happens outside of the awareness of both of you. By bringing this into focus you may access a valuable source of information. Invite the client to pay attention to the two of you and how you are working together. This might be something you do at the end of a session, but for it to inform the exploration you need to do it in the context of the topic. Focus on your working relationship for a few minutes: what does he or she notice about it? Ask how might this resonate with the topic being explored. Alternatively you can offer information about how you are working with him or her that you think might be related to parallel process. This might include sharing how you are being with this client compared to how you are with other clients.

For a long time I could only spot a parallel process after the coaching session through my reflective practice. If this is a new concept for you, try considering this in your reflective practice.

I noticed that I was coming up with lots of suggestions in one session with a client, and I was having to fight the urge to tell her what to do. This was noticeably different to how I am with other clients. Eventually I shared with her my urge to provide her with solutions and it transpired that this was how she felt with the person she was working with. The girl she was talking about never came up with her own solutions and she had to tell her what to do all of the time. She found it really frustrating and wanted this person to take ownership of actions. I invited her to focus her attention on our working relationship and work out what needed to change so that I didn't need to tell her what to do. She then translated this into how she could change to feel the same when working with her colleague.

11. *Challenge and explore ethical issues*

Generally in coaching we don't often hear evidence of illegal or dangerous behaviour in the client's exploration, but you need to be aware of the possibility and consider what you might do if the situation arises. What's more likely to happen is that there appears to be evidence of behaviour that is unethical. What is unethical may be open to question so the steer will come from your own values and beliefs about what you believe constitutes unethical behaviour, or perhaps what you believe the sponsor may perceive to be unethical. You may start in Evident Coach mode by highlighting what you believe is unethical about clients' proposed actions but they may just shrug this off. It's not enough to just highlight the possibility: you need to help them fully understand the consequences if they go ahead with this course of action. In Visible Coach mode you steer them to explore all aspects of the issue and the proposed course of action.

In particular you may ask them what makes the proposed action attractive. What will they get out of it if they do this? There may be other motivations at play that have not yet been surfaced. Also, ask who might be harmed by the proposed course of action. Often unethical activity occurs because the perpetrator has dehumanized those who might be affected, and has possibly not considered fully the consequences for his or her nearest and dearest (for further reading on this subject, see Carroll and Shaw, 2013). Also bear in mind that the motivation behind the proposed action may be legitimate. For example, it might be unethical for a client to 'air the dirty linen' of the company in the tabloids, but there might be something about the 'dirty linen' that needs to be addressed and at the minute the client can see no other way of dealing with it. The means of addressing the problem might be considered unethical, but the issue is legitimate, and therefore needs exploring. Help the client to find another way, or to fully understand all the consequences if this is the only route open to him or her. (The consequences may also include the need for you to break confidentiality.)

12. *Suggest potential solutions*

For me this is a real hot potato of a subject. Should we suggest solutions when we are coaching? Clients often choose coaches because they have a background in their particular field, or have experience of dealing with the same kind of issues, so it's not surprising that the coach can often have ideas about how the client might proceed in particular scenarios. It could make the coaching session so much shorter if we just give clients the answer.

So should we suggest solutions? The answer for me is: it depends on the answers to the following questions: what are you there for? What have you contracted with the client? What is the potential impact if you do it? How does it help the client? What alternative interventions could help the client more? If you are acting as a consultant or mentor then your contract may require you to make suggestions or recommendations.

I believe that making suggestions can limit the client's learning. If the aim for the coaching is solely to find a solution to a problem, then making a suggestion can fulfil this. However, when we tell people what to do, they might not understand why they should do it, or how to carry it out effectively, and as a result they may not get the anticipated result. Also, if it is not their idea they may not be fully committed to it and the solution may fall flat because they do not believe in it. When people come up with a solution for themself they understand why and how they should do it and are more committed to it. Even if we tell clients that they have a choice about the suggestion it can be hard for some to reject the idea: they feel obliged to agree to it. Others are more likely to reject it because it's not their idea, regardless of how good it is!

Having said that, no matter how hard clients look some answers cannot be found within themselves so making suggestions can occasionally have a place in coaching, for example signposting the client to other professional help when it is beyond the scope of the coaching relationship. For me, making suggestions is the last resort. I have to be pretty sure that clients are not going to come up with a better idea for themselves, that it genuinely adds something to the exploration and I am crystal clear about the reasons why I am offering it.

13. Manage the coaching process

When you are managing the coaching process you are in Visible Coach mode. You steer the direction of travel to move the exploration forward and ensure that the session finishes within the time allotted. You are the coaching expert in the relationship. You understand how the process works and how all the various interventions can make a difference to the client. You use this expertise to manage the process. How you manage this process is outside the scope of this book, but there is some further reading on the subject included in the References, further reading and online resources chapter at the end of this book.

Things you may notice

Before you decide to use Visible Coach mode

- The client is in a stressed, agitated, negative or other state that is not conducive to a positive coaching experience.

- You notice an emotional response in the client, or there is an absence of emotional response where you might normally expect to see one.

- You hear assumptions or beliefs behind the client's thinking. You hear statements being made without being qualified and perhaps your automatic response is, 'Why would you think that?'

- You notice a pattern in the client's style of exploration that feels familiar and comfortable and may lead to old ways of thinking.

- You notice aspects that are being avoided by the client – even with using Emergent Coach or Evident Coach mode interventions the client still resists exploring the topic from particular channels.

- Clients seem to be answering a different question to the one you asked, or avoiding the intervention offered. They've changed the subject and started talking about something that is seemingly unrelated, or they start talking using the channel of perception offered but quickly move it to another channel.

- You notice something different about the way you're working with this client compared to others and wonder if it has any bearing on the client's topic.

- Clients talk about actions or express ideas that in your view are unethical, illegal or dangerous. There are aspects of their exploration that give you cause for concern.

After you have used Visible Coach mode successfully

When challenging their thinking you might see evidence of their discomfort in their body language: perhaps they are wriggling in their seat. Or you see a change in their emotional state, for example they may start to become angry or upset. You may notice some agitation in the body language: foot or finger tapping, or crying for example.

Once you have started to explore an emotion you notice clients gaining control of it and continuing with their exploration. They start to explore the aspects of the topic that previously they were missing or avoiding. You hear the links in their exploration to aspects that you have steered them towards.

Often clients will say something like, 'You're not going to let me get away with that are you?' My response is always a version of, 'No, that's what you're paying me for!'

As mentioned before, when they start to think differently you often see a change in their posture and body language. They might change the way they are sitting, for example cross or uncross their legs, or look in a different direction. When there has been a significant shift in clients' thinking you can see it in their whole demeanour. They will sit, stand, hold themselves, look and sound very different to how they did before the change in their thinking.

Inadvertent use of Visible Coach mode

As with all of the modes of presence, you know it is inadvertent use of Visible Coach mode if you use it without it being a deliberate choice. You have not considered other options or why you are choosing it in the moment. All of the following can be inadvertent use of Visible Coach mode.

Commonly I see an avoidance of challenge in coaching: coaches shying away from difficult things that show up, in particular shying away from emotions. When you choose to avoid a challenge you are steering the direction of travel away from the difficult issue; this is still Visible Coach mode. But this time the client may well be missing out on some great learning because of your decision.

At the beginning of a coaching session the client often presents a whole range of aspects that could form the direction of travel. I see many coaches deciding for the client which aspects to explore and which to leave, taking the responsibility away from the client. I have heard coaches say it was really hard to decide which aspect to pick up on in the coaching. If you always or predominantly take responsibility for choosing the initial direction of travel you are steering the exploration.

The coach regularly makes suggestions in the coaching relationship. I would normally expect to make far fewer than one suggestion per coaching session on average. If I find myself making two or three suggestions in one coaching session then I question my motivation for doing so.

The coach disguises a potential solution or recommendation as a question. The question steers the client towards a particular option or solution. An example I heard recently was, 'What extra preparation do you need to do before you see this person again?' There had been no mention of preparation in the lead up to this question but the coach clearly felt that more preparation was the solution.

Often restrictions cause pressure. Coaching sessions are often contracted for one hour or even less sometimes. This gives little room for an in-depth exploration so in the interests of getting finished on time, the coach may well move the exploration on at several points during the session to make sure this happens.

Perhaps clients are taking some time over an exploration, you are getting impatient and you feel the need to hurry them up. You interrupt them to encourage them to move on. I remember one client who seemed to be quite unaware that time was running out, and I caught myself finishing off her sentences in an effort to speed her up! Not good!

Risks

The following are some of the risks associated with using Visible Coach mode:

1 Coach your own needs instead of those of your clients.
2 Bumpy ride.
3 Put clients under too much pressure.
4 Break confidentiality.
5 Cease the coaching.

1. Coach your own needs instead of those of your clients

When using Visible Coach mode we are steering the coaching. We need to be aware that we may steer the exploration in a direction that relates to own needs rather than the clients'. They may talk about a variety of things and you think you heard some emphasis on one aspect but actually the emphasis has come from the fact that it is similar to an issue that you have. These are the hooks that I referred to in Chapter 2.

We are more likely to notice something in our clients if we have a similar issue. That is not to say that it won't be helpful to them to explore this, but you need to check with them when you notice it happening.

2. Bumpy ride

Potentially you are going to be bringing to the fore some difficult emotions, including anger, fear, sadness and hopefully some joy too. Some clients may not be very happy about having their thinking challenged, and get angry.

They may even see it as a questioning of their authority. If you are encouraging them to explore aspects they have avoided in the past this may be very difficult and uncomfortable for them. You need to be prepared to sit with some very powerful emotions. It may be a bit of a bumpy ride for a while and you need to keep yourself grounded to work through it.

3. Put clients under too much pressure

When you are challenging clients' thinking there is the risk that if you are not careful you will move them out of the discomfort zone into the panic zone. No learning can take place in this zone. Remember the trainee abseilers? If you pressure them too much they refuse to budge. There is the potential for the same to happen (metaphorically) in coaching. You need to be able to balance compassion and empathy with challenge.

4. Break confidentiality

A potential outcome of challenging ethics when using a Visible Coach mode intervention is that you may have to break confidentiality. If you are going to do so then you may want to tell clients that you are going to do so. This is a pretty tricky conversation to handle. If you have been courageous enough to challenge their unethical, illegal or dangerous actions and they still intend going ahead, you need to continue to be courageous and consider reporting this. It's at times like this when it's really useful to have a supervisor that you can explore the issue with.

5. Cease the coaching

Highlighting a need for the client to access other professional help may signal the end of your coaching relationship with him or her – at least for the time being. If it is right for the client, this is something that you need to accept gracefully.

Reflective questions

- Read through the list of examples of inadvertent use of Visible Coach mode. When you reflect on your coaching, which do you think are most likely to ring true for your coaching?

- What's your instinctive response when your client gets emotional in a coaching session? Consider a recent time when your client became emotional. What happened? What was the impact on the coaching relationship? What would you do differently given the chance to do it again?

- Consider some of the topics you have recently helped clients to explore. How many of these were topics that resonate with you? Did you recognize this at the time? What happened? On reflection, what would you do differently?

- How does your contracting support you in being able to challenge a client's unethical, illegal or dangerous behaviour? Does anything need to change?

- Has a client ever indicated that he or she is going to take a course of action that is unethical, illegal or dangerous? How did you handle this? On reflection, what would you do differently now? If this has never happened, consider some examples of illegal, unethical or dangerous behaviours that could surface in your coaching. How do you think you would handle them?

- Reflect on one coaching session. How are you being in this session compared to others, either with the same or other clients? How might this be related to the client/s and their topic?

Channels of perception

07

Throughout this book I have talked about opening the client's thinking through a variety of channels of perception about the topic. In all four of the modes of presence the intention is to open up these channels in very different ways:

- *Invisible Coach mode:* you wait while clients explore the topic from their point of view and find their own channels of perception.
- *Emergent Coach mode:* you introduce channels to clients so that they can notice and choose more channels of their own.
- *Evident Coach mode:* you encourage clients to look deeper into their own view using yourself as a channel.
- *Visible Coach mode:* you press clients to consider channels that they have avoided or missed.

There are myriad channels of perception. If you think about the clients' system as having four parts – their work system, family system and their social system encircled by a world system – each part of the whole system impacts or is influenced by the others. None of them stands in isolation. When one part of the system is changed in some way, other parts of the system are affected. Potentially every person in the whole system is a channel of perception. Potentially every person has a different viewpoint. I will call these the 'people channels of perception'.

Then there are the other channels that I will group under the heading 'interpretive channels of perception'. These are the different ways that people can make sense of their systems. We help them to tap into different interpretive channels to facilitate new ways of thinking that help them to use their brain in a different way to what they are used to.

These channels of perception are always available for clients to access but they are not always aware of them. The channels are like radio stations.

Most people listen to just one or two favourites; they are aware of other channels but don't realize just how many choices there are. They choose to listen to the ones they are familiar and comfortable with. To listen to other channels someone has to tune the radio into those channels, or point out their existence.

These two types of channel, people and interpretive, do not form an either/or choice. You are likely to mix them up, using an interpretive channel to explore a people channel. Any one channel mentioned can bring a wealth of information into the client's awareness. To explore this further I will break the two types of channels of perception into subheadings.

First the people channels, which can be grouped into three perspectives:

1 the clients' own point of view;

2 other people who are directly impacted or directly influence the topic, which includes individual, group and collective; and

3 an observer.

I will talk in more detail about these channels, some approaches to stimulate the channels and how your choice of mode of presence may impact on those approaches. Your mode of presence may change as you progress through the approach so expect to vary how you use it as you go through the exploration.

The approaches and channels mentioned in this chapter are by no means an exhaustive list, and I'm certain you will come up with more. I'm not going to explain how the approaches mentioned work: I'm just using them as examples to demonstrate how the various channels can be explored. There are plenty of really great books that cover this diverse range of tools and techniques; those I mention are in the References and further reading chapter.

People channels of perception

1. The clients' own point of view

From this channel clients are looking at the topic from their own point of view. They are only considering the topic in terms of how it impacts on them, what they think about it, how it benefits them, what their desires are. When you use Invisible Coach mode as the starting point, this is probably the point of view that they are coming from. Later you are encouraging them to look deeper inside this channel as they explore their own values, beliefs, assumptions, judgements, behaviours, feelings, emotions and discomfort zones.

Ultimately any changes to be made are the client's own changes as this is the person you are working with. His or her aim may be to influence someone else to be different, but the change facilitated is something within the client so that he or she can achieve this.

Silence

One way of facilitating this channel of perception is through silence, particularly at the outset of the coaching session when the coach is not guiding the coaching in any way. When you are silent clients will guide their own exploration and this will usually follow their own path, or a path that suits their interests and desires. You are giving them time and space to be able to explore the topic for themselves and trusting them to be able to think it through. This is an Invisible Coach mode approach.

Seven-eyed model – mode four

An approach that encourages clients to consider their own channel more deeply is mode four of the seven-eyed model (Hawkins and Shohet, 2012). You are inviting clients to look inwards as a means of exploring the topic. How and what they are thinking and feeling in relation to the topic? What is being stimulated for them by the topic? Who or what are they reminded of? What connections can they make about the topic?

Using the seven-eyed model you use Visible Coach mode to steer clients towards this way of thinking as it's probably not something they will have considered before, then move into Invisible Coach mode while they think about it.

2. *Other people*

This is where the people channels of perception really open up. Every single person in the client's system is a potential channel. Below I will just list some of the people who might have a point of view on the topic, or might be involved in or affected by the topic. You can invite the client to think about what the other person, or group of people, may think about or have to say about the topic, or how they might be affected by it or influence it.

Individuals

Individuals from the clients' work system might include: work colleagues, for example individuals in their peer group or team, other colleagues, their personal assistant, their best customer, a supplier, a competitor. In their family system it might include their spouse or partner, children or grandchildren, parents or dependants. From their social system it might include one or more of their friends or individuals known through their social groups including hobbies, sporting, religious or community groups. These will be people that they know well enough to be able to talk from their point of view.

You are also now part of the clients' system and you may have a point of view about the topic and they may ask for your view. In this case you need to decide whether Visible Coach mode (which is where you are if you offer a point of view) is appropriate for the client in that moment.

Groups

By 'groups' I mean groups of people the client may not know personally as a whole, although the client could be aware of certain members. These groups might be affected, involved, impact, influence or have a view on the topic. Groups include the organization, the team as a whole, other departments in the organization like marketing, customer service, finance, production, distribution, human resources, etc, and customers, suppliers, shareholders, investors, financiers, board of directors, competitors, religious, sport, social or community group members.

Then there are the groups that are slightly removed from the topic. They are not actively involved but may exert some influence over it. These include governing or regulatory bodies, professional bodies, Chambers of Commerce, professional guilds, trade associations or political parties.

Collectives

The third set in the people channels are more amorphous groups. They involve huge numbers of people. The influence or impact of these groups is perhaps more subtle but they can still have a bearing on the subject. Examples include the sector in which the organization sits, the client's profession, indirect competitors (ie those that offer a replacement product rather than the same product), the current economy and politics, country or countries involved including their culture, geographical location or the environment.

3. An observer

The last of the people channels of perception is the interested observer. This is not anyone in particular. The idea is to open up a more objective view of the topic or situation and to help clients to put some distance between them and the topic so that they can see it differently. Often this can be done by inviting them to take a look at the topic as if they were a fly on the wall, or in a helicopter or on a higher floor in a building.

You would never have the time to encourage clients to explore all of these channels. However, inviting them to explore a diverse range of these can prove insightful.

Interpretive channels of perception

The interpretive channels of perception include:

1 symbolism;

2 change of role;

3 physical;

4 language-based;

5 temporal; and

6 analytical tools.

Not everything fits neatly into just one heading. Some channels of perception fit under a range of headings but in the interests of trying to get some order to it I have settled on these.

If you have made a link from the people channels of perception to the three perceptual positions in neuro linguistic programming (NLP – Knight, 2009; O'Connor and Lages, 2004) you might say that these cover every perspective. However, I believe that all the different ways that people can consider a topic are alternative channels of perception.

If you were to explore the topic by systematically going through the people channels this might get a bit tedious, and could result in the client getting into a fixed or familiar way of thinking. This is where the interpretive channels can really help to expand and bring richness to the exploration. The richness in learning comes through using a mix and variety of channels. The interpretive channels of perception are used to open information that is beyond the clients' current awareness by encouraging the client to use their brain differently to access information.

With many of these interpretive channels you may need to use Visible Coach mode to encourage clients to get started or to stay with the particular channel. Because they are often quite different to the clients' usual way of thinking it might feel awkward or uncomfortable and as a result clients stray out of the channel back into their more usual channel. You are likely to use Visible Coach mode to help them to maintain the approach.

You will also use Invisible Coach mode while they explore their answers. I will assume that you will remember this as you read through the following so that I won't keep repeating it.

1. *Symbolism*

Using symbolism is a way of helping clients take a more objective view of the situation, so it can be likened to an observer in the people channels of perception. However, the use of symbolism brings more information into the clients' awareness compared to (for example) taking a helicopter view. The clients' unconscious brain presents more information through the symbols than their conscious brain is aware of. It helps them unearth new information about the topic that they can now pay attention to.

Clients' language is often littered with symbolic language and can easily be spotted. When you are in Invisible Coach mode you might make a mental note of any symbolism heard to reintroduce later in the exploration.

You will often introduce symbolism from Emergent Coach mode where you might invite them to find symbolism to represent the topic. This can be particularly helpful when exploring relationships, whether that's the coaching relationship or the relationship between the client and others in the topic. You can use mode three of the seven-eyed model (Hawkins and Shohet, 2012), and ask a question like: 'If this relationship were a dance (or other metaphor) what would it be?' Then invite the client to explore his or her choice of metaphor.

Most symbolic explorations will start from Emergent Coach mode, as you offer an approach to try to help the clients to explore the topic in a different way while still tapping into their own inner wisdom.

The following are just some examples of symbolism in coaching:

Constellations

A dynamic way of bringing collective groups into the exploration and potentially gaining great insight is through using a constellation or systemic coaching (Whittington, 2012). This is a way of helping the client to explore the wider system and can take account of a variety of individuals, groups or collectives at the same time. It can be facilitated with groups of people; however in a one-to-one situation you can use small objects to represent stakeholders or issues in the system.

You invite the clients to build a constellation that represents the system. You ask the clients to identify objects to represent each of the stakeholders or issues. As they identify each one you ask them to place the object on the table or floor in a place that represents their place in the system. The focus of attention is on the objects and the system and you are basing your questions, statements or interventions on the constellation as it is playing out in front of you. You can use the constellation to explore the relationships between parties involved and use spatial changes to view it from different angles.

This approach will start from Emergent Coach mode. You are offering a way of exploring the topic that will help the client to surface new information and you may need to explain something about the approach before the client can decide whether to participate. Then continue in Emergent Coach mode to help the client to build the constellation by identifying the key stakeholders and aspects and choosing the objects or people to represent these and find the places in the system. As clients do this you move in and out of Invisible Coach mode, remaining silent, watching and observing.

As the exploration of the constellation evolves you may move into Evident Coach mode. You start to share some of the feelings, emotions, words or phrases that you experience that feel like they originate from the constellation.

Finally, move into Visible Coach mode by steering the clients to look at the constellation from different angles. Invite them to view the constellation while standing on a chair or from other parts of the room. At the end of the exploration you use Visible Coach mode to ensure that the clients exit the constellation appropriately. If this is new to you, then before trying it out with your clients I recommend you check out Whittington (2012).

Drawing pictures

Another symbolism channel is drawing. Invite the client to draw pictures or symbols to represent the topic under discussion. Drawing is a way of accessing a whole array of data that is often not accessible through the use of words. You can use it to explore the current situation as it is, or the situation as the client would like it to be. It is a great way of helping clients see more detail in their system. Once started you both focus your attention on the picture that is emerging. Before you move onto exploring the picture, check with clients about what may be missing. My experience is that everything they draw in the picture is significant – it is information that has been drawn from their unconscious mind. It is therefore worth paying attention to everything that is drawn including the location and size of symbols on the page and how these relate to other symbols on the page. Some clients are really happy to draw while others feel a little inhibited about their drawing skills, so some encouragement may be needed to get them started.

Here's how the modes of presence might inform how you progress through this type of exploration. Once clients have got comfortable with the idea of drawing you move between Invisible and Emergent Coach modes until they have completed the picture. From Invisible Coach mode you invite them to talk about the picture, what it represents or what they notice about it. They choose the direction of travel. From Evident Coach mode you make observations about what you notice in the picture, things like: 'I notice that symbol is bigger than this one' or, 'These symbols seem close together compared to these ones' or, 'I notice the differences in colour in the picture.'

From Visible Coach mode you steer the clients to talk about aspects of picture that they have missed or avoided. Sometimes they will try to dismiss aspects of the picture – these are the ones that you may want to steer them to explore in more detail. If the drawing is a representation of the current situation you might choose Visible Coach mode and steer them to think about what they would like to change in the picture, which is a means of opening up potential new solutions for the client.

Artwork

You can also use a piece of artwork to represent the clients' topic, rather than asking them to create their own. Paintings, creative cards, sculptures or any object can be used. (I started using this when a client of mine spontaneously used a mural on the wall to explore her issue.) You explore the artwork in the same way that you would explore a drawing. I carry a variety of artistic prints or creative cards but you can use any artwork that you find around you. The client chooses the artwork to represent the topic and then you ask him or her questions about the artwork to explore the topic.

Clean language

Clean language guides the client in finding a simile to represent the topic. It uses very specific questions made up from the client's own words. The questions are designed to encourage the client to find symbolism to represent the topic and reduce the risk of the coach's own mental clutter or preferences influencing the coaching. It was developed by David Grove in the 1980s (Sullivan and Lees, 2008). If you use this strategy as it was designed to be used, you do not use Evident Coach mode at all: you do not share aspects of yourself.

I offer this 'clean language' example to demonstrate how the modes of presence can be intermingled. The questions are filled with the client's own words, which is an element of Invisible Coach mode, but you are not encouraging the client to explore entirely in free flow. The remainder of the question contains a steer towards a particular way of thinking about the simile, which comes from Visible Coach mode. Exploring a metaphor is an approach that is founded in Emergent Coach mode to widen the client's awareness.

Virtual systems

There are now virtual reality computer systems (see Proreal) that can provide clients with a flexible, changeable view of their system. These enable clients to build a more holographic representation of their system: clients can view their system from multiple angles without having to move out of their chair. They can map out the system and move around and within the system to see if from different perspectives – from different sides, from other people's perspectives and from a helicopter view. They can also change aspects of it to see what difference it would make.

2. Change of role

The next interpretive channel of perception is a change of role. This is where you invite clients to take on a different role in the work you are doing with them. This role can be wearing the shoes of another person in the system, or embodying an aspect of the system, or using a particular strategy to explore the topic. The following are some examples of how you can encourage the client to change roles, or you as the coach can change roles throughout the coaching:

Two-chair work

In this intervention you invite clients to take on two roles: themself and the role of another person or group or an aspect of the topic, for example a problem, a process, a system, the environment – whatever they want to explore.

I believe this has its origins in Gestalt (Bluckert, 2006; 2010). You invite clients to identify a second chair where, when they sit in this chair, they assume the other role. You encourage them to move between the two chairs. In one they speak as if they are the other person in the topic and in the other chair they are themselves. Your role is to facilitate a conversation between the two. You encourage clients to speak from one chair and then move to the other chair to respond and to continue a conversation moving between the two. In their own chair they ask questions or make a statement; they move to the second chair to reply, make statements or ask questions as if they are the other person; and so on until the conversation is completed.

Your original intention in using this as an approach will come from Emergent Coach mode. You are helping clients access more information for themselves through an intervention. You will need to explain what is involved. You are likely to need to use Visible Coach mode to help them to complete the exploration using this approach. Even if they are open to the idea in principle it may take a while for them to be comfortable with the process. It can feel quite alien a) to move between the chairs and b) to speak as if they are the other person. They might be a bit reluctant to move between the chairs to start off with, and they might keep dropping back into talking as themselves rather than as the other person. You might need to press them to move chairs and to stay 'in character'.

Reporter role

In mode one of the seven-eyed model (Hawkins and Shohet, 2012) you invite clients to report on the other person. In chair work they are speaking as if they are the other person; in this channel they are reporting about the other person. What do they look like? What are they wearing? What exactly did they say? What were they doing? Where did they come from? What were they doing immediately before that? What expressions were on their face? What mood were they in? What leads you to believe that?

You invite clients to describe the other person for two purposes: a) to make the other person feel real in the coaching session, and b) to uncover information the clients may have discounted or missed in their exploration. When clients pay this much attention to the other person they often gain significant insights. Here's how it might play out using the four modes:

- *Emergent Coach mode:* you invite clients to describe to you another person in the system, encouraging them to provide you with lots of detail.

- *Invisible Coach mode:* you observe, listen and pay full attention to what is being reported.

- *Evident Coach mode:* you share an image of the person that appeared in your mind while he or she was describing the client.

- *Visible Coach mode:* you have noticed something that he or she has not mentioned about the client and ask him or her to tell you about this.

Personify the problem

In this channel clients take on the personality of the issue (or problem or topic). They give this personality a name and then assume the persona and you interview the persona. This approach originates from narrative therapy and was developed by White (2005) in Australia. It is an approach where clients view a topic as if they are the topic itself, or a problem associated with the topic. You act as an investigative journalist taking two very definite stances to interview the problem. You interview the persona in the way that an investigative journalist might do to get to the truth of the story; this includes using a 'good cop, bad cop' style. It helps if you can add a bit of acting skills to your approach. At first the interview focuses on how and why the persona is successful, building up its ego, asking about what strategies it uses that make it so successful. Then in the journalist role you start to pick holes in the persona's success, finding weak points and trying to undermine the personality. This technique provides powerful insights about how exactly the problem manifests itself and often clients can immediately see new solutions. It can be used to see other people's influence in the topic by asking the persona about what other people contribute to its success and who the people are who can sabotage it.

You are predominantly in Visible Coach mode for this approach. You use and maintain the particular strategy and you are likely to need to encourage the client to remain 'in character' to get the full benefit of the exploration.

Narrator

Invite the client to tell a story. The story can be factual or a representation of the topic, for example a fairy story or a film, or the story of someone famous, and so can be a mix of change of role and symbolism. Clients can tell the story in a variety of ways:

- As an external narrator who plays no part in the story.
- Identify themselves as one of the characters and narrate from that point of view.
- Narrate as if it is one or more of the other characters telling the story.

If they are using a fictional story you can help them to explore how the story is like their topic, as well as how it is different. You can also explore with them how they would like the story to be different, or what advice they would give the characters (Megginson and Clutterbuck, 2005a). In the four modes:

- *Invisible Coach mode:* you listen while they tell the story.
- *Emergent Coach mode:* you ask questions to get them to expand on the story.
- *Evident Coach mode:* you might share how aspects of the story made you feel.
- *Visible Coach mode:* you might steer them to tell the story from the point of view of one particular character.

Investigator roles

In the personification of the problem you were acting out a specific role in the relationship and taking on two very different styles in exploring the topic. These next few approaches are a variation of this. You encourage the client to explore the topic by using a specific strategy for the exploration. Your role is to help him or her to stick with the strategy.

Edward De Bono's six thinking hats In 1985 de Bono (2000) devised a method to help teams to think better together that can be used to help individuals in their thinking. You invite clients to explore the topic while wearing a particular hat (metaphorically or physically). They explore the topic using the strategy denoted by the hat, as follows:

- White hat – focus on relevant data and information; this can be hard facts or rumours.
- Red hat – focus on emotions, feelings and intuition.
- Black hat – focus on critical thinking, finding the holes in the argument, what is right or wrong.
- Yellow hat – focus on the values and benefits, the positive aspects of the topic.
- Green hat – focus on alternative ideas or possibilities, this is the creative hat.
- Blue hat – focus on the process, decide the order of hats and ensure people do not stray out of the current hat thinking.

Clients can choose the order of hat roles, as long as they use all of them at some point and finish with the blue hat.

The Disney creative strategy When Walt Disney and his team worked on their ideas, they went through three very distinct phases before the ideas were finally implemented:

a The dreamer phase, which was when they came up with all their ideas.

b The realist phase, where they developed plans and activities designed to make the dreams happen.

c The critic phase, where they tested out every element of the plan.

If the idea didn't get through all three phases then it didn't happen, or it went back to the drawing board – back to the dreamer phase. You encourage clients to use the three strategies for their exploration particularly to develop potential solutions or actions (see Dilts, 1994).

Appreciative inquiry This is a strategy grounded in positive psychology (Seligman, 2004), this time with four distinct phases:

a discovery;

b dream;

c design; and

d destiny.

The discovery phase is aimed at recognizing and appreciating the best of what already exists and identifying what the client or organization might want more of. The dream phase is focused on possibility and ideas generation and the design phase on deciding what, from their ideas of possibility, they will implement. The destiny phase is focused on how to make it happen. For more about appreciative inquiry see Cooperrider *et al* (2008).

Modes of presence in change of role channels

For these strategy roles your approach might change as follows:

- *Emergent Coach mode:* you offer clients a new way of thinking about the exploration; you provide some guidelines on the use of the strategies.

- *Invisible Coach mode:* they start the approach and explore in the way that they want to. You encourage them by using minimal interventions.

- *Evident Coach mode:* you see them get stuck with a particular aspect and you offer them some knowledge that might help them see it differently.

- *Emergent Coach mode:* you invite them to move to a different location as they start a new strategy for the exploration.
- *Visible Coach mode:* you notice they keep straying out of the strategy so you steer them back to it.

3. Physical

These channels of perception are to do with the physicality in the clients' exploration. Maybe they are thinking too fast, or not fast enough. Maybe there's too much movement or not enough, or you are looking at physical sensations.

Meditation

As I mentioned in Chapter 1, clients need to be quiet and still in their thinking if they are to access their inner wisdom. Sometimes they welcome a few moments of calm – not something they get very often in their busy lives. You might not call it 'meditation' when you offer it to clients: you might offer them a few moments to breathe and calm down or relax. You take them through a few minutes of slow breathing, encouraging them to notice their thoughts and physical sensations and encourage them to let them go. For some clients this may not feel like the right thing to do, so use your own meditative state to facilitate a change in the client. Through being calm and keeping your own breath slow and steady, clients may 'catch' this and calm down with you.

When you do this you are coming from Visible Coach mode. Whether you do it overtly or subtly, you are steering clients to a calmer and potentially more productive state.

Change of place

I've already talked about how the location can have an impact on the coaching. When you want to introduce something new to the thinking, consider moving the location from where clients are viewing the topic, either metaphorically or physically. This may be about helping them look at the topic from the outside in, or vice versa. It can often be about helping clients find some distance from the topic, to take a more detached view. Metaphorical changes of place can include being a fly on a wall, taking a helicopter view or the view from the top floor of the building.

Physical changes might include a change of venue, change of seat, change of position. If you are using approaches like a constellation or drawing for example, clients can get new insights by physically locating themselves in a different part of the room to view what they have created. If using one of the change of role channels, this could be supported by sitting in a different place for each role or strategy.

Walking

Coaching while walking can create a new rhythm to clients' thinking. Often coaching takes place in a seated position, which is not very conducive to movement, yet physical movement can be really helpful in facilitating a change in clients. Walking at different speeds can influence the speed at which clients think and other movement flows more naturally into the coaching. When walking you can build in changes of viewpoint, changes of direction, walking to the top of a hill, stopping points, etc. In fact clients will sometimes change the channel of perception without the need for any intervention from you, for example by choosing to change direction or take a particular fork in the road.

Walking or movement will generally stem from Emergent Coach mode. You are introducing clients to an approach that will help them generate insights for themselves. It becomes Visible Coach mode when you need to press them to introduce some kind of movement.

Somatic

Focus on sensations that clients feels physically in their body. How do they feel the topic? Where do they feel it? What do they feel first? What's the sequence of physical sensations? Exploring the topic in this way can open up information for the client that is in their level three or four awareness. Physical sensations often arise before any thoughts relating to the topic. For example, before someone loses their temper, there will be physical sensations; if clients can recognize the physical sensations in time they have a better chance of curbing their temper.

4. Language-based

The following are examples where the coach uses language as the intervention to inform or change the exploration:

Humour

Encourage clients to see the funny side of their topic. The topics being discussed are often very important and the coaching can become a serious business. Often the best insights follow a really good laugh. The mind relaxes in those few seconds and when the mind is at ease, inner wisdom has the chance to surface.

There is always a grain of truth in wacky, zany or crazy ideas. I often ask for these and then help clients to explore their attraction. Some of the best solutions come from this exploration. Some coaches use highly provocative humour to incite new learning (Knight, 2009). Clients may naturally see the funny side, but often this is more likely to need a steer from you, so this is a Visible Coach mode approach.

The five senses

Try introducing one or more of the five senses as a theme for clients' exploration of the topic. VAKOG is a representational system for how people process information that translates into their language; it is an acronym for Visual, Auditory, Kinaesthetic, Olfactory and Gustatory. Most people will naturally favour one or two of the senses in their use of language. Encourage them to use others. What can they see, hear, feel, smell or taste?

Focus on the clients' language

When you are using this channel of perception you are focusing on the words being used. By doing so you can help clients to explore what is behind their thinking. You are interested in specific words and how they use them; for example:

- Comparisons like 'better than', 'worse than' or, 'clearer than'.
- Generalizations like 'they', 'everyone' or, 'never'.
- Sentences that begin with 'Obviously' or, 'Of course' where perhaps an opinion is being voiced that has not been considered fully.
- Limiters or pressure words, like 'can't', 'should' or 'ought'.
- Indications of movement or lack of movement – eg 'going forwards', 'going backwards', 'flowing' or, 'cutting through'.
- Qualifying words where they appear to have made an evaluation, like 'too much', 'not enough', 'dream team' or, 'worst option'.

This is just a handful of aspects of language that you may show an interest in. Often clients are not aware of the specific language they use nor what is informing the thinking behind it so it can be really useful for them to explore this. For more detailed information about other ways that clients use language, have a look at NLP meta models (Caulfield, 2012) or Charvet (1997).

You are likely to use Evident Coach or Visible Coach mode with these approaches. From Evident Coach mode you might observe that you notice particular aspects of clients' language. From Visible Coach mode you question them specifically about the language; for example, 'Who do you mean when you say "they"?'

5. *Temporal*

Most clients arrive for coaching immersed in either past or present events whereas the coaching is often focused on the future. They are preoccupied with something they have done, or the multitude of things they should be doing. There is much to be gained from exploring aspects of the past or the present before considering where to go in the future. Understanding what has happened in the past, or the full current situation can provide insights about what needs to be different for the future. The temporal channels of perception are therefore: past, present, now, future and age.

Past

Sometimes focusing on past events will provide an understanding of what needs to be different going forward. Taking time to explore an event for which clients would have preferred a different outcome, might help them to work out new strategies for dealing with similar issues in the future.

Sometimes things that happened in the past are still preventing things from moving forward. Kohlrieser *et al* (2012) talk about how grief impacts on organizations if it is not dealt with. People who have left the organization, redundancies, divisions closed, mergers, takeovers, rebranding, etc all cause losses that people need to come to terms with. A significant question relating to the past is: what has happened in the past that needs to be acknowledged, before we can move on to the future?

Present

The present needs just as much focus (if not more than) the future. Logic may dictate that of course we know what the present looks like, but often there is a lot of information in the present that is outside of our awareness. And awareness of this information can make a big difference to options moving forward. At the beginning of the chapter I talked about how all parts of the system are interrelated and impact and influence all the other parts. If the client is not aware of how all these parts interrelate in the present, any planning for the future is potentially distorted.

Often clients go from one goal to the next without celebrating or even acknowledging their successes. Sometimes it's helpful for clients to take stock of their current successes and how they achieved them. Helping them to acknowledge and celebrate success provides a firmer foundation for their next step.

Now

I know that 'now' is the present but I want to make a finer distinction here. The present relates to what may be happening anywhere in the current system, but the timeframe can range from days to hours. Focusing on *now* means focusing on what is happening in this moment: encouraging clients to think about what is happening for them physically and what they think in this moment. What is happening right now, right here? What is the client feeling right now? What is he or she thinking right now? How does this relate to the topic?

Future

Outside of the coaching sessions clients will often have given only a cursory glance to the future before they're sucked back into the present. The reason they have engaged you is usually because they want something to be different in future, but most clients have not thought this through fully. Covey (1989) recommended that we start with the end in mind. I find that exploring the desired future will often open up insights into new behaviours and thinking even before any of the 'real' coaching gets started. There are quite a few future-related questions that can be used to open up future-based thinking including:

- What does the world of tomorrow need from you (Hawkins and Smith, 2006)?
- What will you want others (or yourself) to say about this topic in one year, 10 years, 50 years, 100 years?
- When you look back from any of these points in time, what will you say/think?
- What will you know in a year's time that you don't realize you know now?

Age

Age is a slightly different temporal channel of perception that feels more personal. Future age-based questions might be:

- What will people say about this at your funeral?
- What do you want to be able to say about this when you retire?
- When you are 80 years old what do you want to say about the difference your work on this topic has made?

Often more significant insights can be gained by asking the client to take a child's perspective. When clients have children or nieces and nephews you can ask what they would make of the topic. Or you could ask, how will this impact on your grandchildren? What will this mean for your grandchildren when they reach your age?

It can be just as powerful to encourage clients to remember and go back to their own childhood: what would they have wanted to say as a child of seven, to the grown up person that they are now? What advice would they give themself if they were still only seven?

Also consider encouraging clients to use the parent, adult, child ego states from transactional analysis (Stewart and Joines, 1987) as a means of exploring the topic.

6. Analytical tools

The last section of channels of perception relates to the analytical tools that can be used as a basis for the client's exploration. I'm not going to explain them here but here's just a few:

Ishikawa's Cause and Effect model, often known as fishbone analysis (1990).

Forcefield analysis (Cantore and Passmore, 2012; Swanson and Creed, 2013).

SWOT analysis (CIPD, 2010).

SOAR analysis – an alternative to SWOT based on appreciative inquiry (Lewis, 2011).

Service design processes (Design Council; Stickdorn and Schneider, 2011).

Quality improvement processes, like Lean or Six Sigma (George *et al*, 2005; iSix Sigma; Womack and Jones, 2003).

Business competition analytics like Porter's five factors of competitive position (Porter, 2008).

PESTLE analysis (CIPD, 2010).

GROW model

I'm going to finish by mentioning the GROW model, developed by Whitmore (2009), because this is a model for coaching that most coaches are familiar with and I can use it to demonstrate the complexity of these channels of perception and how they intermingle.

The GROW (Grow, Reality, Options and Will) model is a structure for a coaching session (other structures are available!) You can use it as a process to steer the coaching and it offers four strategies for the exploration. You do not use the GROW model in isolation. You will use a whole range of other approaches, while remaining within the structure and the strategies. You will have an overall strategy of goal setting (for example), but you will use other approaches and interventions before you finish with this strategy. The four GROW strategies fit with the change of role channels of perception, but all of the channels of perception can fit in with GROW. The same goes for many of the channels of perception I have mentioned.

Reflective questions

- What channels of perception are missing, if any, from your coaching? How might including these channels in your coaching impact on your clients? What do you need to do next to be in a position to introduce this as a channel for your clients?

- What approaches do you use currently in your coaching? Consider one of them from the point of view of each mode of presence. How is your use of the approach different for each mode?

- When you learn a new approach for your coaching, consider it in the context of the four modes of presence. Which of the four modes might this be most suitable for (if any)? How would you use the approach in that mode? If you change modes (pick one) what will be different about how you use this approach? Repeat for each mode.

A journey of self-discovery

08

If you are reading this book then I imagine you have a desire to develop your coaching practice. If you are anything like me, you want to be the very best coach that you can be. Tomorrow I will always want to be a better coach than I am today. You may be wondering where to go next in your development and I hope that this chapter can help a little with that decision.

Developing your coaching practice is a journey of self-discovery. Self-discovery is at the heart of being the best coach that you can be. It is a journey of challenge, richness and doubt. You will challenge yourself to gain a richness of learning and through that challenge there will be times of doubt. If we don't doubt ourselves sometimes we are missing out on some key learning opportunities. At these times we are in our discomfort zone – embrace it and the profound learning that you can gain.

There is not just one route to becoming the best coach that you can be. Coaches come from all walks of life and every single coach's journey is different. One of the joys of the coaching profession is the wide diversity of development opportunities available, but this can also be a dilemma. Because there are so many different routes it can be hard to decide which path to choose. It really doesn't matter which route you take: most routes will take you to where you want to be. The important thing is to get on a path, take a step and keep walking! When you come to a crossroads or a fork in the road, choose the path that feels right for you.

Lifelong learning

The coaching profession is evolving. Compared to many professions it is relatively new, having only been recognized as a profession for about 40 years or so – although I'm sure coaching has actually been taking place since mankind could speak!

The profession itself is still learning. There is a growing amount of research that has links to or is directly about the field of coaching. Almost every day there is something new published on the subject, all of which can help us to understand and develop our coaching. There is research in the fields of neuroscience and psychology, new philosophies and ways of thinking, research about what makes coaching effective, new tools and techniques being introduced; the list goes on.

Over time I have come to realize that my learning about being a coach is not going to come to an end. The more I learn, the more I realize just how much more there is I want to learn. This can be represented by a balloon – a balloon that will never pop! The air inside the balloon is the learning you have achieved, the air that surrounds it is the potential for learning, the balloon skin is the window to what is available to learn. As the balloon fills up with air, the balloon skin stretches, the window becomes larger and we can see more of the opportunities for learning.

If we stop learning then my belief is that eventually we become limited in how much we can help our clients. So I see that the path to being the best coach that I can be means that this will be a lifelong journey. This is a journey that I very much welcome and look forward to enjoying.

Increase self-awareness

Self-awareness is fundamental to being able to differentiate between and use the four modes of presence. It is critical to your coaching presence. To be able to help others to tap into their own inner wisdom you must first be able to do this for yourself. You develop your self-awareness to enhance your ability to help others.

I discussed what I mean by self-awareness in Chapter 2, and I talked about some of the personal factors that might impact or influence your coaching. The only way that you can prevent any of these factors having an impact is if you are aware of them and deliberately take action.

What you learn to help you in your coaching is likely to help you learn more about yourself. Often when learning you will act as a client so that someone else can practise their coaching skills. These are valuable opportunities to increase your self-awareness. Whatever you learn that will develop your coaching skills, take some time to consider these in the context of your self-awareness. For example, if you learn about aspects of transactional analysis, how does what you have learnt show up in your coaching, as well as your life and relationships, and what might you do differently specifically in your coaching as a result of this learning? What follows in this chapter are ways to develop your self-awareness.

Mindfulness and meditation

My definition of mindfulness is: staying present in the moment, paying attention and being very aware about what you are doing and why you are doing it. It is the underlying theme of the four modes of presence. You will often hear the words 'mindfulness' and 'meditation' being linked. Mindfulness can be developed through meditation but you need to bring the mindful state that you cultivate through meditation into your coaching practice. Meditation helps you to quiet your thoughts and still your mind, which is the state you need to be in to access your inner wisdom, your own invisible coach. I came to meditation relatively late in life and I wish I had found it earlier. Learning to meditate has made a pivotal difference in my coaching presence and in my life.

After meditating most people feel calmer and more grounded. They are more resilient and are better placed to handle anything that might come their way. In your coaching practice, meditation skills can help you to let go of your mental clutter more easily and create time and space in the moment to consider your options more fully. It can help you to stay grounded and work through any tension that may arise. You can also use meditation skills to help your client to become calmer and more grounded. The difference can be tangible, as demonstrated below.

I was running a two-day group workshop that straddled a weekend. During day one, I found one of the delegates difficult to deal with. He had his own agenda for the day. I felt that he was trying to sabotage everything I did and he was really stretching my patience to the limit. By the end of the day I was agitated and so were the rest of the group. Feedback indicated that a couple of people were considering not coming back for day two because of it. I was not looking forward to day two.

Over the intervening weekend I had been fortunate enough to secure a place on a spiritual retreat (run by the Brahma Kumaris – see the Appendix). At the retreat I experienced a weekend of looking inwards and learning how to meditate. I learnt how to stay in the moment and gain a sense of calm and a feeling of being grounded. I learnt how to tap into this calm and grounded state periodically throughout the day.

Day two of the workshop was completely different. The group was the same, he was the same. I was different. He arrived with the same agenda, but this time I was able to maintain my calm state throughout the whole day. As the day progressed he calmed down and became more amenable and the group was calm and relaxed. In the feedback they commented that day two was much calmer and less stressful than day one. The power of meditation skills and mindfulness was reinforced for me that day. Not only did it make a difference to me, it made a difference to 10 other people in the room and I was the only person who knew what had made the difference!

There are a growing number of opportunities available to learn mindfulness or how to meditate. There are plenty of books on the subject including ones that relate specifically to mindful coaching (Hall, 2013). There are short courses that combine mindfulness with other coaching or therapeutic interventions like mindfulness-based stress-reduction courses or mindfulness-based cognitive coaching (also see Hall, 2013). There are lots of short meditation courses available. Some of the religious and spiritual orders offer meditation classes for free or for very low cost including Buddhist and Brahma Kumaris centres across the UK. The Brahma Kumaris regularly offer free conferences specifically aimed at coaches that combine mindfulness and meditation practices with coaching. Keynote speakers have regularly included some of the well-known names from the coaching profession including Sir John Whitmore (2009) who developed the GROW model.

Reflective practice

I see reflective practice as central to developing self-awareness, presence and your coaching practice. Being quiet and reflective enables you to tap into your own inner wisdom. I am referring here to the practice of formally reflecting on each coaching session, ideally within a few hours while it is fresh in your mind. You reflect on how you worked with the client, what went well, what didn't work so well, what interventions you used, what other options were available to you, paying particular attention to what mental clutter or personal factors (Chapter 2) impacted or influenced your coaching and how might you work with this or other clients differently next time.

Reflection is more than just thinking about the session. For me just thinking about it is like trying to see a ball of string spinning in your head. All you can see is the outside of the ball. You want to see the string but to do so you need to take hold of it and pull it out, then you can see as much of the string as you like. You can't do that while it is spinning around. Writing a reflective piece is like taking hold of the string and gradually pulling it out of your head so you can see it. As you write you access more data about the coaching session than you can when just thinking about it. Commonly I use writing, but I also draw or use objects as a system for my main reflection, completing this with a written conclusion.

However you complete your reflection, by the end you need to have drawn some conclusions, learnt something about yourself or your coaching and/or have an intention to do something different as a result. If you are new to this you could start by writing in free flow. Just write whatever occurs to you at the time. Let the words flow on to the page. Write something, anything. It's helpful to write from three perspectives – your own, your client's and an impartial observer. When you have finished ask yourself these three questions: What? So what? Now what?

The learning from the reflective practice will be strengthened if you use a structure and I also suggest that it is useful to change your structure periodically so that you don't get drawn into the same thinking process every time. As you learn to use different coaching models and techniques, use these as a template for your reflective practice. Use a model or a tool or technique that you might use with a client and ask yourself the same questions that you would ask him or her. Use different models that will encourage you to use different perspectives in your reflection.

Here is my offer of a structure, based on the learning in this book, to use in your own reflective practice. You can find material on other structures of reflective practice in Brockbank and McGill (2012), Cameron (1992), Hay (2007), Mezirow *et al* (2009) and Moon (2004). As you become more accomplished at reflecting on your practice in hindsight you will find that you are able to reflect on your practice while you are still coaching (Schön, 1991).

Reflective practice structure

Allow yourself some time after a coaching session to complete the following; write down your answers:

- Choose one point in the coaching session. Which mode of presence were you in?

- Describe what happened.
- What worked well at this point?
- Why did you choose that particular intervention at the time?
- What was the story you were telling yourself at the time?
- What value, belief, assumption or judgement might have informed your choice?
- What other personal factor (from Chapter 2) may have informed this choice?

Now consider the same point in the coaching session from the clients' point of view of:

- What happened?
- What was the story they were telling themselves?
- How did the intervention impact on them?
- Which mode of presence would they say you were in?

Now consider the same point in the session from a fly on the wall perspective:

- What would a fly have observed happening?
- What factors would the fly observe impacting or influencing the coaching?
- What would the fly say about the impact for the client?
- Which mode of presence would the fly say the coach was in?
- Which mode of presence do you now believe you were using?
- How does this compare to your answer to the first question?

Conclude your reflection. What conclusions do you draw from this reflection? What will you do differently next time?

Record coaching sessions

It's amazing what you can learn by recording and playing back at least some of your coaching sessions as part of your reflective practice. Video or audio both work well for this. Audio recording can feel less intrusive for the client, at least at the beginning of the session, but most clients quickly settle down no matter which you choose. Only record your sessions with permission from the client and after you have established clear boundaries about how you will use the recording and what you will do with it when you have finished.

Play back the recording and write your reflections within 24 hours if you can. When you do it in this timeframe, you can still remember what was going on in your head at the time of the interventions. This makes it easier to reflect on how your own personal factors might be showing up in your coaching. At least once try writing a reflection about your session before playing it back. Then listen to the recording and observe how your memory of it differs to what actually happened. You might be very surprised. Recording your coaching sessions is a good way of finding out what you really do in your coaching!

Listen to the part of the recording that you have just reflected on:

- How does hearing or seeing the recording compare to your recollection of it?
- The recording will jog your memory of what was going through your mind at the time. How does that compare to your memory of it?
- How does this affect your reflection?

Alternatively, try this approach when you have recorded the session:

- Guesstimate how much time you spent in each mode of presence during the session.
- Watch or listen to the whole recording. While you are doing so, try to keep a tally of each time you went into each mode. It won't be an exact science, but a rough tally will be sufficient.
- What proportion of your time was spent in each of the modes? How does this compare to your guesstimate?
- Did you spend more time in any one of the modes in particular? Which mode did you spend the least amount of time in?
- What conclusions might you draw from this?
- What might you do differently next time?

Therapeutic interventions

I feel that when talking about developing your self-awareness I must mention therapy. It is important to me because I made a significant leap in developing my self-awareness through a period of therapy. I am not a therapist so I can only talk about this from the point of view of having been a client of therapy for several months.

A few years ago I hit a wall and was not functioning well. I came to a standstill at work and was signed off for three months with depression. I knew this wasn't something I was going to fix by myself so I sought help from a counsellor. The person was registered with the British Association for Counselling and Psychotherapy (BACP) and I now know that the counsellor took a person-centred approach to my therapy.

This is what I learnt about the benefits of therapy. I learnt about what had shaped me to become the person that I was then. I learnt about strategies that I had developed in childhood and how I was still using them in adulthood. I got to understand some of the baggage that I was carrying around with me; how it was getting in my way and sabotaging my aspirations. I started to understand some of my outdated beliefs and to reframe these into more enabling ones. I recognized some of the baggage for what it was and learnt to deal with it. I learnt to let go of some thinking that was holding me back and become more proficient at handling the mental clutter that remained. I questioned what and why I did things and developed new ways of behaving that have helped me to get what I wanted in life. It helped to rebuild my confidence and got me back onto a good path. I came out of it emotionally stronger and more self-aware than I had ever been previously.

All that I learnt about myself through therapy would have been influencing or impacting on my coaching, outside of my awareness.

When I use the word 'therapy' I am talking about an intervention that helped me to work through a depressive state and included a deep exploration of my thoughts, feelings and behaviours and their origins. Like me, many people don't access therapy until they have hit a wall. If you have never hit a wall and/or never been in therapy, I wonder how much baggage you might be carrying with you that you are not aware of. How much of a difference would it make if you were to explore yourself in this way?

There are a number ways to do this without having to go through therapy. Some coaches or supervisors have a psychotherapy background and therefore may be able to help. Or you could undertake training in one of the therapy fields as part of your coach development. These usually require students to experience therapy as part of the training.

Supervision

Supervision is an extension of your reflective practice and helps to take your reflections to a much deeper level.

When I first decided to work with a supervisor I had no idea how I would benefit. All the coaching professional bodies, certain books (Hay, 2007) and my course tutors recommended supervision, but in truth I couldn't see why I needed it. However, I decided to heed the advice and try it out. I found a supervisor and it was one of the best development decisions I have made. I know now that I will continue to work with supervisors for as long as I am a coach. It is an essential part of my development.

I think many coaches are not clear about what supervision is and why they should access it. The word itself can be off-putting, suggesting a managerial role or a hierarchy, or that the coach is not fully trained or capable. But supervision is none of these. First of all it is a supportive, equal relationship, not a hierarchy. Coaches who access supervision are usually highly capable and want to continue developing their coaching practice. It provides a supportive environment to enhance your coaching. The focus in coach supervision is the coaching relationship: what is happening for you, the client, between the two of you and in the wider system. It brings to your attention information that is currently outside of your awareness. While you can explore problems or issues in your coaching, you learn as much from exploring coaching relationships that are going well.

Here's what I find are the benefits of engaging with a qualified coach supervisor. It helps to:

- Identify when my personal factors are impacting on the coaching; deepen my self-awareness, and enhance my ability to keep these out of coaching relationships.
- Recognize what assumptions and beliefs are impacting on my coaching.
- Recognize when transference and counter-transference are impacting on coaching relationships.
- Objectively view my coaching practice; reviewing the coaching practice to a much greater depth than is possible through individual reflective practice.
- Look beyond the coach client relationship and recognize what other influences may be in play.
- Recognize when ethical issues may be showing up in the coaching and help to work out how to address these.
- Open up new or different ways of working with clients.
- Ensure that I am not absorbing any toxicity or negativity that may arise through the work; it can help to prevent burn out.
- In summary, it helps me to see what I cannot currently see (Bachkirova, 2013).

Supervision builds on your own reflective practice by providing a heightened, deepened and broadened exploration.

Here's an analogy for supervision: You bring to the session a trawler-size fishing net all bundled up. The net is not working quite as effectively as you want it to. You think you might know the cause but because it's all bundled up you can't be sure. With the help of the supervisor you lift and stretch the net out so that you can see the whole thing. Now you can see all the holes, the tears, the snags, the stuff that's caught up in the net and you can immediately see what's limiting its effectiveness and what to do about it. The cause is never what you originally thought it was!

Engage with a coach

Do you have a coach or engage in coaching on a regular basis? Apart from all the obvious benefits it gives you the opportunity to gain new insights for your own coaching practice. One of the main benefits is that it acts as a reminder about how it feels to be a coaching client. When you have been coached, take some time to reflect on what worked well for you as the client and what this might mean for you in your coaching practice.

In Chapter 2 I mentioned some diagnostic tools that are designed to provide insights about ways of thinking, feeling and behaving and what influences these. You might consider engaging a coach who is qualified in the use of one or more of these tools to help you to develop your self-awareness about how these factors might impact or influence your coaching.

I undertook quite a few diagnostic tools throughout my career but it took a while for me to make the connection between what I learnt about myself and the impact it might be having on my coaching. I made the mistake of accepting the diagnostic information as 'this is who I am'. I learnt about how others might be different so that I could be more tolerant of these differences. What I didn't see at the time was the opportunity to learn how to 'be' different. I didn't realize the extent to which I can choose to be something different. I've revisited some of my earlier learning in the context of how this impacts on my coaching and how I want to be different.

If you engage a coach to help you through the use of a diagnostic tool, focus specifically on what this means for your coaching. If you engage with a coach who has a different coaching background, or uses a different field of coaching, you can see this in action and it may suggest an avenue for your own development.

Practise your coaching

Learning to coach is the same as developing any other complex skill. Most complex skills need to be practised quite a bit before you reach a reasonable standard. If you want to get really great at something you need to keep on practising. Top sportsmen and accomplished musicians don't just turn up on the day and expect to do better: they practise for hours, refining and honing their skills to become masters of their art. The same principle applies if you want to become a really great coach.

Find a way to regularly practise your skill. There are coaching practice forums all around the UK, which provide a space where coaches of all levels of experience get together specifically to practise their coaching skills. They coach and observe each other using new and existing skills. The main focus is on learning about coaching practice. Coaches may have read about or learnt new skills, models or techniques and they bring them to the forum to try them out in a safe environment before launching them on their 'real clients'! Coaches learn from seeing how other coaches work with clients and there is rich learning from each other. Coaches give and receive feedback about their coaching practice.

If you can't find a forum close to you, you could set up your own group, perhaps with some of your coaching colleagues or fellow students from courses you have attended together. These forums or groups are an ideal place to practise any learning that you might gain from reading this book. Try practising each of the four modes separately at a practice forum. Explain the mode you are using and ask observers to notice and provide feedback to you about how you use it. The Association for Coaching – www .associationforcoaching.com – offers co-coaching forums all over the UK.

Develop your own style

Typically coaches are taught skills, but over time how these were taught and how you actually use them become very different: coaches start to develop their own approaches. You are no longer learning a profession, you are developing your art. Any new learning that you take on board will enable you to keep on developing in your own unique way. You take on board new information, new ways of thinking, new learning, new tools and techniques and you mould and reshape these, take bits out, put bits in and then intertwine these into your coaching practice. The greater the variety of learning you undertake, the more eclectic the mix of interventions you can draw on. The more you learn, the greater your ability to be flexible and creative with your clients. This increases the chances of your coaching having a transformational effect on your clients. Any learning will help you to develop your own unique style.

Tap into other fields of expertise

In my previous career I undertook a wide range of learning including leadership and management, problem solving, marketing, project management and accounting, and I have been surprised by how many tools relating to other fields I have been able to incorporate into my coaching. For example, I have used tools that are traditional problem-solving tools, or leadership models, to help clients explore their topic in more detail. Sometimes it has helped just being able to talk in a language that the client understands. It's possible that whatever learning you have undertaken throughout your career can be adapted and used as a coaching tool.

If you do not have this broad base of learning there may be advantages to attending courses that cover these types of aspects; examples include leadership, entrepreneurship, marketing, process improvement systems, creative design and project management. All of these include tools and techniques that you may use to support the client's exploration and discussion. Some of these skills will also stand you in good stead if you are running your own business.

Qualifications

Something that you may be considering for your coach development is further qualifications. At the moment there is no requirement in the industry for coaches to be qualified. The professional bodies do not require qualifications although your membership is limited if you have not undertaken training with a coach training provider. More courses are being accredited by the coaching professional bodies, and undertaking these courses will help to smooth your way to coach accreditation (discussed next). Some clients are not interested in qualifications, all they want to know is – can you help me? It can depend on the size of business you want to engage with. The bigger the business the more likely you are to be asked for qualifications.

Some people coach without ever having had any training – if there's no professional or client requirement for an academic qualification, why bother? The answer for me lies in the level of learning you can achieve while you are working towards your qualification and the difference it can make to your confidence and the quality of your coaching. Higher-level qualifications, for example a Master's degree, move you towards a more critical analysis of your coaching practice to deepen your knowledge. You understand better what works with clients and why. You understand yourself better, what might get in the way of your coaching and as a result your confidence increases and you are better equipped to achieve transformational change with your clients. The courses usually offer a structured pathway through a range of aspects linked to coaching, opening your eyes to the wide diversity of learning that is available. Often the learning is based on leading-edge research introducing the latest developments in neuroscience, psychology, leadership, etc.

One last point on the subject of qualifications. Currently the profession is self-regulated: at some point in the future, it may become regulated – it has been talked about for some time. If this happens there may be a requirement to hold some form of qualification in order to establish a coaching practice.

Accreditation

Membership of one of the coaching professional bodies is an element of the self-regulation in the industry. All of these bodies offer accreditation as a voluntary option for coaches. It is designed to encourage coaches to aspire to high quality standards and to provide a measure of assurance to the buyers of coaching. The same companies that might ask for qualifications might also require coaches they employ to be accredited by one of the professional bodies.

From a coach development perspective, the level of scrutiny that you apply to your coaching practice to become accredited can provide a significant learning opportunity. The process makes you think about what you are doing, how you are doing it and why – the same things that I am suggesting you pay attention to in your reflective practice.

Key principles for coach development

- Self-awareness is a key aspect of coaching presence. Find ways to understand yourself more deeply, and then review this learning in the context of how it might impact or influence your coaching.

- Reflective practice is a key aspect of developing self-awareness and coaching presence. Complete a structured reflection after every coaching session.

- Supervision will considerably enhance the benefits of reflection. Both supervision and reflection will increase your ability to keep your personal factors from influencing your coaching.

- Coaching is an evolving profession. We are learning more and more about how the human mind works, so as coaches we need to keep up with the new learning.

- Broaden the range of coaching interventions in your repertoire. Learn about different coaching styles. Having more tools available enables you to be more flexible and adaptive to your client's needs. It helps to increase your options across the four modes of presence.

- If you want to be a great coach, regularly practise your art. Make practising your coaching skills an integral part of your continuing professional development.

- Practise mindfulness and meditation to bring a calmness and grounding to your coaching presence.

- Make learning a lifelong commitment. It will help you to continuously develop your invisible coach so that you are better equipped to help others to surface and strengthen their own invisible coach.

Reflective questions

- Has this chapter highlighted any gaps in your journey that you might want to explore?

- How much impact is your reflective practice having on your coaching practice? What needs to change in your reflective practice to enhance its effectiveness?

- Now that you have finished this book, consider three things that will help you to develop your coaching presence.

- Which of these would have the most impact on your coaching?

- What is the first step that you will take to develop this aspect?

Enjoy your ongoing journey.

APPENDIX

Glossary

analogy Symbolism incorporates analogies, metaphor and similes. The word 'metaphor' is often used instead of 'simile' or 'analogy'. The difference between the three is quite subtle. An analogy is a comparison between two things that might be similar in some way. For example the production manager role and the HR manager's role both involve moving resources around. *See also* metaphor and simile.

client This is an overarching word used to describe any of the following: the person who is being coached (whether paid or unpaid), the customer or the supervisee.

metaphor A metaphor is using something different, perhaps a symbol or an object, to represent something else. For example I talk about this stone as if it is me. *See also* simile and analogy.

paraphrase When paraphrasing you are trying to tell the same story that the client has told, but using your own words. You interpret what he or she said into different words that mean roughly the same as what you think the client has said.

parking Noting a potential topic or aspect that the client mentions, but which you do not raise in the moment. You make a mental note of it to come back to later if needed.

personal factors Anything that may be influencing or impacting on your coaching that relates to you and your life experience (see Chapter 2).

self-awareness Defined in Chapter 3.

simile A simile is drawing a likeness between two very different things, for example coaching is like gardening. *See also* metaphor and analogy.

stakeholder Anyone who may be affected by the client's topic, and is in his or her wider system. See 'People channels of perception' in Chapter 7 for a list of who these people might be.

summarize When summarizing you pick out what you interpret as some of the key points in the client's exploration. You are using the client's own words. You repeat back a series of sentences that the client has used to sum up what you think he or she has told you. You are telling the same story that the client has told using the same words.

topic The subject, problem or issue that is being discussed in the coaching session.

Coaching professional bodies

In this section I reference information from the three main UK coaching professional bodies. This will be done in alphabetical order of the coaching bodies, which are:

- The Association for Coaching (www.associationforcoaching.com)

    European Mentoring and Coaching Council (www.emccouncil.org)
- International Coach Federation (www.coachfederation.org.uk)

Each chapter in this book can be used to develop aspects that the three bodies have determined are best practice for coaches. The extracts are taken from their competencies unless otherwise stated.

Introduction

The learning about coaching presence, maturity and guiding beliefs reflects the following aspects.

Association for Coaching

(The first two are extracts from the Coach and Executive Coach Accreditation Scheme Overview, Master Coach/Master Executive Coach level):

An expert knowledge and deep understanding of coaching practice, a strong theoretical and practical underpinning and an awareness of coaching related disciplines (psychological models, coaching supervision, mindfulness, etc).

A coaching approach that draws on a broad range of models, tools and techniques, tailored to individual requirements and demonstrated in action.

Is optimistic for and encourages self-belief in the client.

Accepts the client 'as is' and believes in the client's potential and capability.

European Mentoring and Coaching Council

Proactively manages own 'state of mind' to suit the needs of the client. (74)

Accounts for moment by moment decisions during their practice. (97)

Adapts approach/technique in the moment in response to client information . . . .(107)

International Coach Federation

Coaching Presence – Ability to be fully conscious and create spontaneous relationships with the client, employing a style that is open, flexible and confident.

Is present and flexible during the coaching process, dancing in the moment.

Attend to the client and the client's agenda and not to the coach's agenda for the client.

Sees many ways to work with the client and chooses what in the moment is most effective.

1. Laying the foundations

The learning in this chapter relates to the following.

Association for Coaching

Agrees a formal coaching agreement with client and all stakeholders . . . .

Establishing a trust-based relationship with the client.

Establishes a high level of rapport . . . .

European Mentoring and Coaching Council

Proactively manages own 'state of mind' to suit the needs of the client. (74)

Establishes an ethically based coaching/mentoring contract . . . . (79)

International Coach Federation

Understands and effectively discusses with the client the guidelines and specific parameters of the coaching relationship . . . .

. . . come to an agreement with the prospective and new client about the coaching process and relationship.

Ability to create a safe, supportive environment that produces ongoing mutual respect and trust.

2. What's impacting on your coaching?

The learning about the factors that can impact and influence your coaching reflects the following.

Association for Coaching

Remains focused on the agreed client agenda and outcomes.

Acts on own critical reflections and client feedback to improve coaching practice.

European Mentoring and Coaching Council

Identifies when their internal process is interfering with the client work and adapts behaviour appropriately. (35)

Critically reflects on practitioner paradigms and their impact on clients and client systems. (98)

Builds self-understanding based on a range of theoretical models and structured input from external sources with rigorous reflection on experience and practice. (73)

Continuously reviews, reflects on and updates personal beliefs, attitudes and skills to improve their coaching/mentoring. (75)

International Coach Federation

Attends to the client and the client's agenda, and not to the coach's agenda for the client.

I will be aware of any issues that may potentially lead to the misuse of my influence . . . .

3. Invisible Coach mode

Developing your skills for using Invisible Coach mode will help with the following.

Association for Coaching

Pays close attention to the client, staying fully present and engaged.

Demonstrates effective listening and clarifying skills and differentiates between what is said and what's left unsaid.

Inspires the client to identify and implement self-directed learning opportunities.

. . . yet working from the mind-set of knowing little.

European Mentoring and Coaching Council

Demonstrates a high level of attentiveness and responsiveness to the client in the moment . . . . (104)

Listens at a deeper level. (83)

International Coach Federation

Is open to not knowing and takes risks.

Helps clients to discover for themselves the new thoughts, beliefs, perceptions, emotions, moods etc that help their ability to take action and achieve what is important for them.

4. Emergent Coach mode

Developing your skills for using Emergent Coach mode will help with the following.

Association for Coaching

. . . elicit new insights . . . .

Helps broaden a client's perception of an issue . . . .

. . . develops the client's ability to self-coach.

Takes a systemic approach to coaching the client, encompassing the complexities of multiple stakeholders, different perspectives and conflicting priorities.

European Mentoring and Coaching Council

Remains impartial when encouraging the client to consider alternatives. (60)

Uses a range of techniques to raise awareness, encourage exploration and deepen insight. (81)

Applies a systems perspective to building understanding and insight. (86)

International Coach Federation

Sees many ways to work with the client and chooses in the moment what is most effective.

... help the client understand from another perspective ....

... shift their viewpoint ....

... evoke discovery, insight ....

5. Evident Coach mode

Developing your skills for using Evident Coach mode will help with the following.

Association for Coaching

... using self and personal reactions to offer client feedback ....

Uses 'self' as a resource for the development of the client's self-awareness and learning by offering 'here and now' feedback.

Provides observational feedback where relevant, leaving the client free to choose to act upon it or not.

European Mentoring and Coaching Council

Attends and works flexibly with the client's emotions, moods, language, patterns, beliefs and physical expression. (80)

Remains impartial when encouraging the client to consider alternatives. (60)

Uses a range of techniques to raise awareness, encourage exploration and deepen insight. (81)

International Coach Federation

Accesses own intuition and trusts one's inner knowing – 'goes with the gut'.

Communicates broader perspectives to clients and inspires commitment to shift their viewpoints and find new possibilities for action.

Expresses insights in ways that are useful and meaningful for the client.

Helps the client identify and access different resources for learning.

6. Visible Coach mode

Developing your skills for using Visible Coach mode will help with the following.

Association for Coaching

... tackling difficult conversations with the client ....

Provides relevant information and feedback to serve the client's learning and goals.

Asks questions to challenge client's assumptions, elicit new insights, raise self-awareness and gain learning.

Helps broaden a client's perception of an issue and challenges to stimulate new possibilities.

European Mentoring and Coaching Council

Identifies clients who may have an emotional or therapeutic need which is beyond their professional capability to work with safely. (101)

Recognizes when clients have a need outside of safe and contracted boundaries and takes appropriate action. (103)

Uses feedback and challenge effectively to increase awareness, insight and responsibility for action. (82)

Uses language to help client reframe or challenge current thinking/ understanding. (85)

Enables significant and fundamental shifts in thinking and behaviour. (106)

International Coach Federation

Demonstrates confidence in working with strong emotions, and can self-manage and not be overpowered or enmeshed by client's emotions.

Reframes and articulates to help the client understand from another perspective what he/she wants or is uncertain about.

Invokes enquiry for greater understanding, awareness and clarity.

Challenges client's assumptions and perspectives to provoke new ideas and find new possibilities for action.

7. Channels of perception

This chapter offers insights to potential new learning and fits with the following aspects.

Association for Coaching

Helps broaden a client's perception of an issue and challenges to stimulate new possibilities.

European Mentoring and Coaching Council

Synthesizes insights derived from extensive exploration of theoretical models and personal evidence. (96)

Seeks relevant themes, ideas and models to explore and develop their practice. (77)

Connects various models and new ideas into their own model. (93)

International Coach Federation

Promotes active experimentation and self-discovery . . . .

Ability to ask questions that reveal the information needed for maximum benefit to the coaching relationship and the client.

8. A journey of self-discovery

All three of the main coaching professional bodies talk about continuing professional development in their Code of Ethics. In addition, each of them includes information on the subject of developing self-awareness. The following are extracts relating to this.

Association for Coaching

Actively reflects on coaching practice and outcomes.

Acts on own critical reflections and client feedback to improve coaching practice.

Participates in regular coaching supervision to reflect on, and improve, practice.

You are expected to regularly seek consultative support, typically from a qualified and experienced coach supervisor . . . . (taken from the Code of Ethics and Good Practice).

European Mentoring and Coaching Council

In the EMCC two of the eight competence categories are 'Understanding Self' and 'Commitment to Self-Development', both of which directly relate to this topic. Just a few of the individual statements include:

Critically reflects on practitioner paradigms and their impact on clients and client systems. (98)

Invites feedback from peers by demonstrating their practice before them. (100)

Participates in regular supervision in order to develop their practice. (38)

Builds self-understanding based on a range of theoretical models and structures input from external sources with rigorous reflection on experience and practice. (73)

Demonstrates own unique approach to coaching/mentoring . . . . (109)

International Coach Federation

I will at all times strive to recognize personal issues that may impair, conflict or interfere with my coaching performance or my professional relationships. Whenever the facts or circumstances necessitate, I will promptly seek professional assistance and determine the action to be taken . . . .

REFERENCES, FURTHER READING AND ONLINE RESOURCES

Association for Coaching (2012) (accessed 10 April 2013) *AC Competency Framework*, http://www.associationforcoaching.com/media/uploads/accreditation-documentation01/Coach_Competency_Framework_AC_.pdf

Association for Coaching (2013) (accessed 10 April 2013) *AC Coach and Executive Coach Accreditation* scheme overview, http://www.associationforcoaching.com/media/uploads/accreditation-documentation01/AC_Coach_Accreditation_Overview_12_12_.pdf

Association for Coaching (accessed 10 April 2013) *Code of Ethics and Best Practice*, http://www.associationforcoaching.com/pages/about/code-ethics-good-practice

Association for Coaching (accessed 14 July 2013) *What is Co Coaching?* http://www.associationforcoaching.com/pages/events/co-coaching-forums/what-co-coaching

Bachkirova, T (2013) 3rd International Conference on Coaching Supervision

Back, K and Back, K (2005) *Assertiveness at Work A practical guide to handling awkward situations*, 3rd edn, McGraw-Hill, Maidenhead

Belbin (accessed 14 July 2013) http://www.belbin.com/

Bluckert, P (2006) *Supporting people through change – A Gestalt perspective* in *psychological dimensions of executive coaching*, pp 117–45, McGraw-Hill Open University Press, Maidenhead

Bluckert, P (2010) The Gestalt approach to coaching, in (eds) E Cox, T Bachkirova and D Clutterbuck, *The Complete Handbook of Coaching*, pp 80–93, Sage, London

Brahma Kumaris (1995) *Living Values: A guidebook*, Brahma Kumaris World Spirituality University

Brahma Kumaris (accessed 14 July 2013) Residential Retreats, http://www.globalretreatcentre.org/retreats/residential-retreats

Briggs Myers, I and Myers, P B (1980) *Gifts Differing: Understanding personality type*, Davies-Black Publishing, New York

Brockbank, A and McGill, I (2012) *Facilitating Reflective Learning: Coaching, mentoring and supervision*, Kogan Page, London

Buckley, A and Buckley, C (2006) *A Guide to Coaching and Mental Health. The recognition and management of psychological issues*, Routledge, London

Cameron, J (1992) *The Artists Way. A spiritual path to higher creativity*, Putnam, New York

Cantore, S and Passmore, J (2012) *Top Business Psychology Models. 50 Transforming ideas for leaders, consultants and coaches*, pp 181–4, Kogan Page, London

Carroll, M and Shaw, E (2013) *Ethical Maturity in the Helping Professions: Making difficult life and work decisions*, Jessica Kingsley, London

Caulfield, M (2012) *The Meta Model Demystified. Being a simple and jargon explaining introduction to the NLP meta model* (Kindle edition)

Charvet, S R (1997) *Words that Change Minds. Mastering the language of influence*, 2nd edn, Kendall/Hunt Publishing, Dubuque, IA

CIPD (2010) (accessed 14 July 2013) *SWOT analysis. Resource summary*, http://www.cipd.co.uk/hr-resources/factsheets/swot-analysis.aspx

CIPD (2013) (accessed 14 July 2013) *PESTLE analysis. Resource summary*, http://www.cipd.co.uk/hr-resources/factsheets/pestle-analysis.aspx

CIPD (2013) (accessed 14 July 2013) *The psychological contract. Resource summary*, http://www.cipd.co.uk/hr-resources/factsheets/psychological-contract.aspx

Clutterbuck, D and Megginson, D (2010) Coach maturity: An emerging concept, *International Journal of Mentoring and Coaching*, 8 (1)

Cooperrider, D L, Whitney, D, Stavros, J M and Fry, R (2008) *Appreciative Inquiry Handbook. For leaders of change*, Berrett-Koehler, San Francisco, CA

Covey, S R (1989) *The 7 Habits of Highly Effective People*, Simon and Schuster UK, London

Csikszentmihalyi, M (1990) *Flow. The psychology of optimal experience*, Harper, London

Csikszentmihalyi, M (2004) Flow, the secret to happiness, *TED Ideas worth Spreading*, http://www.ted.com/talks/mihaly_csikszentmihalyi_on_flow.html

de Bono, E (2000) *Six Thinking Hats*, 2nd edn, Penguin, London

Design Council (accessed 14 July 2013) http://www.designcouncil.org.uk/about-design/Types-of-design/Service-design/What-is-service-design/

Dilts, R B (1994) *Strategies of Genius: Volume 1: Aristotle, Sherlock Holmes, Disney, Mozar*, Meta Publications, Capitola, CA

European Mentoring and Coaching Council (2008) (accessed 10 April 2013) *Code of Ethics*, http://www.emccouncil.org/src/ultimo/models/Download/4.pdf

European Mentoring and Coaching Council (2009) (accessed 10 April 2013) *Competence Framework*, http://emccaccreditation.org/wp-content/uploads/2009/10/Competence-Framework-Oct-20092.pdf

Flaherty, J (2005) *Coaching Evoking Excellence in Other*, 2nd edn, Elsevier Butterworth-Heinemann, Oxford (there is now a 3rd edn)

George, C (2009) (accessed 14 July 2013) CIPD, *The Psychological Contract: Managing and developing professional groups (Work and Organizational Psychology)*, http://www.cipd.co.uk/hr-resources/factsheets/psychological-contract.aspx

George, M L, Maxey, J, Rowlands, D T and Price, M (2005) *The Lean Six Sigma Pocket Toolbook. A quick reference guide to 70 tools for improving quality and speed*, McGraw-Hill, Maidenhead

Goleman, D (2007) *Social Intelligence. The new science of human relationships*, Arrow Books, New York

Hall, L (2013) *Mindful Coaching. How mindfulness can transform coaching practice*, Kogan Page, London

Hawkins, P and Shohet, R (2012) *Supervision in the Helping Professions*, 4th edn, Open University Press, Maidenhead

Hawkins, P and Smith, N (2006) *Coaching Mentoring and Organizational Consultancy: Supervision and development*, Open University Press, Maidenhead (new edn now available)

Hay, J (2007) *Reflective Practice and Supervision for Coaches: Coaching in practice*, McGraw-Hill Open University Press, Maidenhead

Honey, P and Mumford, A (1986) *The Manual of Learning Styles*, Pearson, Oxford

International Coach Federation (2008) (accessed 10 April 2013) *Code of Ethics*, http://www.coachfederation.org/ethics/

International Coach Federation (accessed 10 April 2013) *Core Competencies*, http://www.coachfederation.org/credential/landing.cfm?ItemNumber=2206&navItemNumber=576

Ishikawa, K (1990) *Introduction to Quality Control*, 3A Corporation, Tokyo

iSix Sigma (accessed 14 July 2013) http://www.isixsigma.com

Kimsey-House, H, Kimsey-House, K, Sandahl, P and Whitworth, L (2011) *Co-Active Coaching. Changing business and transforming Lives*, 3rd edn, Nicholas Brealey, London

Kline, N (1999) *Time to Think. Listening to ignite the human mind*, Ward Lock, London

Kline, N (2009) *More Time to Think. A way of being in the world*, Fisher King, Wharfedale

Knight, S (2009) *NLP at Work: Neuro Linguistic Programming: The essence of excellence*, 3rd edn, Nicholas Brealey, London

Knowles, M S, Holton, E F and Swanson, R A (2011) *The Adult Learner. The definitive classic in adult education and human resource development*, 7th edn, Elsevier Butterworth-Heinemann, Oxford

Kohlrieser, G, Goldsworthy, S and Coombe, D (2012) *Care to Dare: Unleashing astonishing potential through secure base leadership*, Jossey-Bass, San Francisco, CA

Kolb, D A (1984) *Experiential learning. Experience as the source of learning and development*, Prentice-Hall, Upper Saddle River, NJ

Lewis, S (2011) *Positive Psychology at Work. How positive leadership and appreciative inquiry create inspiring organizations*, Wiley Blackwell, Oxford

Maslow, A H (1943) A theory of human motivation, *Psychological Review*, 50 (4) pp 370–96

Megginson, D and Clutterbuck, D (2005a) My story, in *Techniques for Coaching and Mentoring*, pp 81–3, Elsevier, Oxford

Megginson, D and Clutterbuck, D (2005b) *Techniques for Coaching and Mentoring*. Elsevier, Oxford

Mezirow, J, Taylor, E W and Associates (2009) *Transformative Learning in Practice: Insights from community, workplace, and higher education*, Wiley, Chichester

Moon, J (2004) *A Handbook of Reflective and Experiential Learning: Theory and practice*, Routledge Falmer, London

O'Connor, J and Lages, A (2004) *Coaching with NLP. A practical guide to getting the best out of yourself and others*, HarperCollins, London

Passmore, J (2006) *Excellence in Coaching: The industry guide*, Kogan Page, London

Porter, M (2008) (accessed 14 July 2013) The Five Competitive Forces that Shape Strategy, *Harvard Business Review*, January, http://hbr.org/2008/01/the-five-competitive-forces-that-shape-strategy/ar/

Proreal (accessed 14 July 2013) http://www.proreal.co.uk/

Rooke, D and Torbert, W R (2011) *7 Transformations of Leadership* in *HBR's 10 Must Reads on Leadership*, pp 137–62, Harvard Business School Publishing, Cambridge, MA

Schofield, R (2009) Growing the learner from within: deep learning through experiential and reflective events, *International Journal of Mentoring and Coaching*, **2** (2)

Schön, D A (1991) *The Reflective Practitioner. How professionals think in action*, Ashgate, Aldershot

Seligman, M (2004) The new era of positive psychology, *TED Ideas worth Spreading*, http://www.ted.com/talks/martin_seligman_on_the_state_of_psychology.html

Starr, J (2008) *The Coaching Manual. The definitive guide to the process, principles and skills of personal coaching*, 2nd edn, Pearson, Oxford

Stewart, I and Joines, V (1987) *TA Today. A new introduction to Transactional Analysis*, Lifespace Publishing, Melton Mowbray

Stickdorn, M and Schneider, J (2011) *This is Service Design Thinking: Basics, tools, cases*, Wiley, Hoboken, NJ

Sullivan, W and Lees, J (2008) *Clean Language. Revealing metaphors and opening minds*, Crown House Publishing, Bancyfelin, Carmarthen

Swanson, D J and Creed, A S (2013) *Sharpening the focus of force field analysis*, in press

White, M (2005) (accessed 14 July 2013) *Externalizing Conversations Exercise*, Dulwich Centre, Australia, http://www.dulwichcentre.com.au/michael-white-workshop-notes.pdf

Whitmore, J (2009) *Coaching for Performance: GROWing people, performance and purpose*, 4th edn, Nicholas Brealey, London

Whittington, J (2012) *Systemic Coaching and Constellations. An introduction to the principles and practices and application*, Kogan Page, London

Whitworth, L, Kimsey-House, K, Kimsey-House, H and Sandahl, P (2009) *Co-active Coaching: New skills for coaching people towards success in work and life*, 2nd edn, Nicholas Brealey, London

Womack, J and Jones, D (2003) *Lean Thinking: Banish waste and create wealth in your corporation*. Simon & Schuster UK, London

INDEX

Also available from **Kogan Page**

Also available from **Kogan Page**

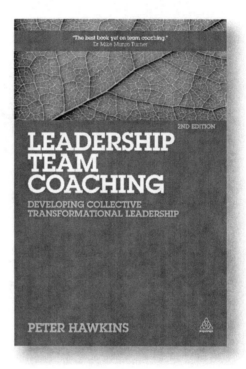

CPSIA information can be obtained at www.ICGtesting.com
Printed in the USA
BVOW05s0037060314

346842BV00004B/12/P